Negot

Learn How to Negotiate for Greater Business Success, and Avoid Mistakes

(Master Tips and Strategies for Work, Love, Friendship and Business)

James Wardell

Published By **Phil Dawson**

James Wardell

Negotiation: Learn How to Negotiate for Greater Business Success, and Avoid Mistakes (Master Tips and Strategies for Work, Love, Friendship and Business)

ISBN 978-1-77485-638-3

Legal & Disclaimer

The information contained in this ebook is not designed to replace or take the place of any form of medicine or professional medical advice. The information in this ebook has been provided for educational & entertainment purposes only.

The information contained in this book has been compiled from sources deemed reliable, and it is accurate to the best of the Author's knowledge; however, the Author cannot guarantee its accuracy and validity and cannot be held liable for any errors or omissions. Changes are periodically made to this book. You must consult your doctor or get professional medical advice before using any of the suggested remedies, techniques, or information in this book.

Upon using the information contained in this book, you agree to hold harmless the Author from and against any damages, costs, and expenses, including any legal fees potentially resulting from the application of any of the information provided by this guide. This disclaimer applies to any damages or injury caused by the use and application, whether directly or

Table Of Contents

Chapter 1: Learning How To Assert.......... 1

Chapter 2: Strategies For Influence And
Persuasion. 9

Chapter 3: Classic Styles Of Negotiation 21

Chapter 4: What Makes Negotiation
Possible?... 32

Chapter 5: How To Negotiate A Buyer ... 45

Chapter 6: Negotiation Techniques........ 50

Chapter 7: Negotiating For Your Benefit 66

Chapter 8: The Process Of Negotiation .. 73

Chapter 9: Presenting A Case 81

Chapter 10: Characteristics Of Negotiation
.... 83

Chapter 11: Clever Psychological
Buyer/Seller Negotiation Tricks............ 102

Chapter 12: Getting The Groundwork In
Place Early... 116

Chapter 13: Types Of Negotiation In
Corporate.. 127

Chapter 14: Setting The Agenda 137

Chapter 15: Daily Exercise Benefits...... 146

Chapter 16: How To Avoid Screwing Up A
Negotiation 152

Chapter 17: Probing The Other Side's Case
.... 156

Chapter 18: Negotiation Strategies...... 166

Chapter 19: Negotiating With Your Boss
.... 176

Conclusion 182

Chapter 1: Learning How To Assert

This chapter will discuss the importance to be assertive. You will also learn how assertive and dominant you can be.

You must be assertive to be a successful negotiator. It is essential that you can communicate clearly and effectively with others to get the best deal.

What is assertive behaviour?

It is not always easy to discern assertive behavior. As a negotiator you need to understand the fine line between being assertive or aggressive. People sometimes confuse this line, and end up being aggressive rather than assertive. Because of this, we believe it is important to understand how to differentiate between both types of behavior.

Balance is key for assertiveness. You need to find a balance in your negotiations. To be assertive in your dealings, you must have the right balance. It is important to understand your needs and wishes, as well the needs of those around you. An assertive person has self-assurance, but is fair with empathy. If you treat others without empathy and fairness, you can easily fall prey to aggression.

Aggressive Behavior - It's all about Winning. Aggressive behavior focuses on winning and not worrying about being right or wrong. Being aggressive means that you only do what you believe is right for you. You can be a little selfish and disregard other people's needs, wants, and desires. Apart from being selfish, you are also pushy and bully people to reach possible conclusions. You are quick to take what you want, and not take the time necessary to ask the right questions.

Imagine a boss coming to your cubicle just five minutes before you are due and throwing all the work they have to do. This is what you call being aggressive. They want to achieve the best outcome for their clients without worrying about how it will affect your rights and feelings. The opposite is true for bosses who give you work and tell you that you need to complete it before noon tomorrow.

Benefits of Being Assertive

As you'll learn, assertiveness can have many positive effects. You will see the best of yourself, and you will appreciate what you can offer.

The benefits of assertiveness can be enjoyed at the workplace as well as in other areas of our lives:

Make Great Managers. The best managers are assertive. This is because they treat people with respect and fairness. A strong manager will have the ability to communicate with employees in a way that is respectful and fair. They are often loved and seen as leaders in even roles that do no give them the authority to lead.

Negotiate Effectively. Negotiating successfully can be achieved by being assertive. Not only will you get the best result for you, but your assertiveness will allow you to look at other perspectives and develop a strategy that works for both of them. If you are assertive, you can quickly understand both your opponent's and also your own position.

Better Problem Solvers. The best problem solvers are those who feel confident and empowered. Before you made a decision, have you been guided by pessimistic thoughts? But assertive people don't go through that.

Are Less Anxious. As assertive people are more confident, they tend to feel less anxious than the rest. Certain situations don't make assertive people feel threatened or victimized.

How to be More assertive

Before we go into detail about how you can assert yourself in your life, we must warn you that it isn't an easy process. Through this phase, you will have make difficult decisions and have to consider possible solutions. If you have the right amount, it can pay off in the long run and be a worthwhile investment.

Your Rights are Important

Assertive people are able to understand and respect their rights. In order to be assertive, you need to understand your rights and value them. Every person has their own unique value and they can add to the group or organization. To claim your rights, you need to first understand what value you have and then work to improve it.

The self-confidence or self conviction that you have in yourself, and your value, is what will help you be assertive in your life. The entire belief process will allow you to see that you are worthy respect and dignity.

Be aware that your self confidence should not be mistaken for self importance. Self importance can be aggressive as it encourages you not to place others' needs and feelings on a pedestal. You need to know that your rights matter just as much as those of other people, and that they are not superior to yours.

Confidently Communicate Your Needs and Desires

If you're confident that your priorities (or your wants) will be met by the negotiation process, you can only negotiate to your potential. As a negotiator and a person trying to navigate life, it's important that you understand your personal needs and want and don't leave them up to others.

Take some time and identify what you want or need now. You can set goals and accomplish them.

If you are clear about what you want, then you'll be better able put your desires on the table. If you believe your needs and wants can be met, then it's time to stick to what you want. All reasonable desires and needs should be addressed. If you feel that you have a valid need, but the request is not feasible right now you should politely ask whether it can be done in a year or six-months.

Recognize the fact that you don't have control over other people

We tend to be influenced by those around us. Anybody outside of our control is not included in that circle. Identify your circle. You have to realize that you cannot control the behavior of people around you.

While assertiveness can be viewed as a feeling of responsibility for others' actions, it does not include an attitude of assertiveness. Your assertiveness should be contained. You must also remain calm. You have the ability to control and influence your own behavior. You cannot dictate the behavior of someone else, and you certainly can't ask them to act in a certain fashion.

It is possible to change your behavior, but it is best to do so in a consistent manner. Don't worry about other people changing your behavior.

Express yourself

A positive attitude is a key part of being assertive. You should be able express yourself without sounding or being negative.

You must be open and honest about whatever you are feeling, even if this is something you find difficult. It is essential that you bring up the stressors in your life constructively and should be discussed.

Don't be afraid expressing your opinions. Be open to all the opposition that you encounter, and be willing to let your true emotions out. It is important not to get too emotional or show disrespect. Respecting others is essential even when you feel that you are not being met. It is possible to control your emotions and take charge of things.

Chapter 2: Strategies For Influence And Persuasion.

We have already discussed the importance likability and creating a personality that is attractive in the first chapters. The skills and techniques described in the previous chapter are just the tip. These are the essential tools to help you get through your daily life. They are extremely powerful but not very general. The first step to a pleasant personality?

This chapter will focus on some extremely effective strategies for negotiation. Once you've created a personality that people are comfortable with, the next step will be to learn how expert strategies can be used to negotiate, compromise, and influence.

Conflict resolution theories refer to the PIN framework as a way to understand conflicts.

According to the thesis, conflict manifests on three levels.

* Positions

* Interests

* You have to be able to do it.

These are the different stances that people take on different issues. These statements are about the side or position you take on a particular issue. Positions are the most visible manifestations of differences on an topic.

Interests refer to the outcome people would like to see after negotiations. Interests reflect the motivations behind the positions taken. They can be harder to trade than positions because they are deeper than those of the position.

They are non-negotiable and unassailable conditions or values that prevent a person, party or organization from functioning. Fundamental and essential needs are critical.

PIN framework allows you to successfully negotiate any situation. Because it analyzes and understands both the visible and hidden aspects of a problem, it is a wonderful tool to help you navigate your way through it. Problems often appear difficult because most people start by stating their positions. But if you use PIN to get people to give up their positions in favor of their real interests, you can exchange tokens and start to negotiate with one another on the same problems that seemed so difficult a few months ago.

Roger Fisher (internationally acclaimed negotiation theorist) and William Ury (author of 'Getting To Yes') state that successful negotiation involves focusing on relevant interests, needs, and value.

However, interests and need often go hand in hand. Negotiation experts can help you distinguish between the two. John Burton, a resolution expert suggests that interests represent positive conclusions and needs are essential conditions that people can function without.

Understanding the interplay between positions, interests, and needs is key to directing any deal to your best outcome.

2.2 Understanding Different Currencies for Negotiation

In negotiation-speak, "currency" is any item that can be traded. It could include positions on a subject, political opinions as well as authority and power. A currency basically refers to anything that is up for negotiation, discussion, or trading.

Any trade-off is not just about one side. Negotiations are all about trade of recognized tokens, as well creating and identifying new trade-offs.

Great negotiators understand how to maximize what they have. It's possible to get the results and energy you desire by keeping your attention on the primary currency. But you might have to compromise more than you wish. Because trade-offs require you to give and take, it can prove extremely helpful to learn to see beyond the lines.

While the other side is focused solely on the obvious, you should seize the chance to learn more about the currencies that are used at work. It will help you distinguish between the student positions of other students and their actual interests. Once you understand this, you can capitalize on your newly discovered currencies and gain an edge.

You might be involved in a realty deal where the obvious currency of exchange is the price. If this happens, you should take a step back. Is one party pressing for quick settlement? Do they seem eager for a quick resolution? If so then money might not be the only issue. However, it could be that time is an important factor. You can leverage the vulnerability of the other party on a less obvious topic and use it for trades on the one you care about most. In exchange for a quick sale, you might be able to negotiate on matters of money more than they realize.

It's all about understanding your strengths and using that knowledge in order to affect the outcome. While it might seem like you are starting and ending on the same currency, as with pricing in the above example, you can manipulate the results by using other factors (such as urgency and time) to your advantage.

This is how average people are distinguished from greats. It's all about keeping your eyes open for any potential wiggle-room in negotiations. It's true that the only hand you can have is the one dealt to you, but it's worth looking at the cards of other parties to see if you can win.

2.3 Understanding Emotions and How to Use Them

It might seem counterintuitive to discuss emotions in order to achieve your goals after having discussed sincerity.

But the best negotiators are aware that winning negotiation and persuasion does not mean giving people what it wants. Instead, they help people reimagine what it is they want.

If you can read people, this is the only way you will be able to achieve it.

To give people what they want, or at least convince them of it, you must first know what they want. Remember the PIN framework.

Understanding people's emotions can help you gauge their behavior. If you are able to read and understand the emotions of people, you will be able guess their needs and predict their reaction in most situations. This knowledge can prove invaluable in negotiations.

2.4 The Power Of Empirical Proof

If you have statistics and numbers on your side, it is easy to impress others and bring them around.

Claims that can be statistically backed up are much more plausible than those that cannot. Your chances of convincing people are much lower if there are graphs, statistics and other scientific tools that can be used to support your argument.

There is something so satisfyingly satisfying about scientific evidence that people almost find it impossible to resist its charms. You need to be able to demonstrate your worth to a potential client and to give your advantage over your competitor. If you want people trusting you enough to invest in you, then you need to be more persuasive than your words.

The first thing that you will probably think of when you hear about the Law Of Scarcity is your high school Economics class. The concept is simply that the modern global society has greater needs and wants than what the world and its limited resources can provide.

Negotiations basically involve offering something to the other party that they do not have access to, in return for something you would like. People must make decisions between multiple options and prioritize when there is scarcity.

You might now wonder, "How is this different from trading the old-fashioned way?"

The key is that you have the upperhand because you are able to offer something important, rare, or valuable. It is easy to see that whoever has all the resources has all the power. So if your resources are unlimited, you can instantly control the negotiations.

2.6 Don't speak on your own: Let your record speak.

Even though there are more stakes and bigger ramifications to political discussions than in all other negotiations it is unfair to assume that this doesn't apply to other situations. You will have to adjust your methods. You must be careful when you are negotiating business deals.

Your record should speak for itself in business negotiations.

Yes, there will be times when you have to present information to potential clients and customers. A successful negotiator knows the difference between being proud about what they have accomplished and being conceited. If you're bidding on a prospective client's contract or trying negotiate a rate, it's important to have all references, testimonials and customer reviews.

2.7 Homework

It is impossible to succeed in life without being prepared for the many milestones and difficult tests that it presents. The same goes for negotiations. You'll be blindsided if your research is not done properly.

You still need something to go on. Great negotiators know how to change and adapt quickly. This means you have to be fully informed about the situation, the parties, and all possible outcomes.

It will help you to create an action strategy, predict future behavior, and be prepared for anything. It will also help you be more prepared and empower you to come up with alternative strategies and backups, so you aren't caught off guard under pressure.

Remember, knowledge IS power!

2.8 Aim For A Win-Win Situation

If you go into negotiations looking to win a contract, you will be disappointed.

Yes, there are times when we refer to "winning at negotiations" in this ebook. However, it's important for everyone to understand that a successful negotiation is not about one side winning, but all parties.

Your attitude is the single most influential factor in the process. It influences how you behave and communicate, how much information you get, how you handle problems, whether you collaborate with others, or whether you stand alone.

Your attitude is going to have an effect on the outcome. Your attitude will affect the outcome of negotiations. Make it a point that you strive for a win/win scenario. Don't look for a win against another party. Instead, make it your mission find a solution fair to everyone.

If your intention is defeat, you will cause problems. If your intention to cooperate, then you will solve them.

2.9 Have a plan, set your limits

Try to ignore the other side of negotiations.

Negotiations can only be a benefit to those who come prepared to handle everything. Your plan will ensure you stay on the right track and won't be distracted by any unexpected or unexpected developments that might occur during negotiations.

The planning process includes determining what you want from negotiations, making decisions about compromises, and choosing your preferred style of negotiating - all before you start.

If you have a plan in place for negotiation and you know your limits, you will be more confident and can meet your goals. Even if you have the need to adapt your strategies and change your techniques during negotiations, your plan can help you keep your eyes on your ultimate goal.

Chapter 3: Classic Styles Of Negotiation

This chapter will be about the classics and how they relate to negotiation styles. Negotiators have a range of negotiating styles. The style they choose to use is often a reflection of who they are. You can choose to use different styles for experienced negotiators. These "situational" negotiators are able to see the whole arena and choose the most appropriate style for their particular situation. They choose another style if the current one is not effective.

The context of the negotiation is what will determine which style works best. As I go through four different styles, you can think of the best situation in which each style would work.

The Dominator and The Dictator

This style is easy for you to identify. This is a style of control, dominance, and dominance. They will dominate the conversation and dictate the agenda. They are usually very loud and can be challenging. They make you feel uncomfortable and insecure from the start. Dominators expect and elevate assertiveness.

This style "bowls" you over. They might feel that this is a way to make an impression on the people they represent.

Dominators are typically on a roll. They often have to be around less assertive types. Their team usually includes people who can take a "backseat" and let their dominators do their thing.

Although they can be helpful with people who feel less confident or weaker, this style is not recommended for maintaining long-lasting relationships. They communicate in a straightforward manner and are quick to reach a conclusion. They will intimidate their opponents and use challenging speech as a way to "turn the tide" against them.

Dominators use tactics to ask you if you were serious about the deal. They can be very proud. The Dominator can be very smug if their opponent pulls out of the deal.

They can be stopped. The simple "Are they finished?" or "I like how you are impressing yourself but you don't impress me." Let's go back and examine why we're here.

The Avoider-The Retirer

Retreaters do not like confrontation and strong disagreement. They do not enjoy a lot of verbal problem-solving. It is preferable to pass the proposals between the parties and give the paper directly to the other side. They avoid developing a relationship or friendship with the other party and their discomfort is obvious. They might use this style to protect themselves from being seen as weak or ineffective if they are under pressure. Although it's more difficult to deal with than the Dominator style, this one is less objectionable. I like to use three strategies when using this style. I focus quickly on the "bottom line". What is your best offer. What is the minimum you will pay? What do you need to get from this? This brings me closer toward the area that we can agree. There are two other strategies I use: "Expand" or "Contract" the negotiations' scope.

If I expand the scope of the negotiations, I enter territory that Retreater had not anticipated. I move the negotiations off of my proposal paper and because it wasn't expected. People should always be able to work on your proposal, if possible. Because this was not anticipated, the objection that my proposal is only for consideration doesn't apply. Contracting the scope works exactly the same.

To solidify an agreement, make small concessions and increase their willingness. These types tend to stick to more traditional structures and less innovation for agreements. They are less adventurous and more prone to fear "outside of the box" thinking.

I speak softly and in very conciliatory voices. When they reject my proposals I say, "I regret that wasn't acceptable. Let's see if there is something that can work for us all."

You might get frustrated if the Retreater has no power to negotiate and is just a messenger. Avoid the game, not the player. Let's take, for example, the car dealership. Some dealerships create a sales team with a strong, intimidating sales leader and a bunch of retreater sellers. The retreater is there in order to exhaust you. The deal maker is then given you, once you're fully tired. You are called a "closer" by this sales manager. He will explain to you how the sale person got you this sweetener. You would be foolish not accept it. You won't find another deal like this. Even as I write this, it is getting to me.

The Compromiser and the Accommodator

When the circumstances are right, the Accommodator might be a joy to deal with. Accommodators strive to please, and they are always willing to make concessions or tradeoffs. They value relationships. It would be easy to look at this and say, "That is great!" Some situations are impossible to solve with compromises. Because it is too easy to make concessions for the sake or goodwill and not in your best interest, some negotiations should not be done this way. Accommodators love that the idea of dividing the difference is possible if they can't agree. Splitting the difference sounds fair. But it is rarely a decision you should make. I will speak more about this in the book.

Accommodators tend to count the number of concessions but rarely recognize that not all concessions have equal value. If this is something you are used to, I'm sorry. Don't lose sight of building a relationship with your client and being liked, rather than making the sale. Clients who have a tendency to do this are my concerns. Although they are respected and enjoy working with their partners in negotiations, they can often make disastrous agreements.

The Problem Solver, The Collaborator

Collaborator is a type of problem-solving approach that focuses on making sure everyone wins. Their problem-solving mindset makes them results-oriented. This style is quick to build trust and respect because it uses a problem-solving approach. This is a good way to negotiate with partners. This works both in business and in labor relations. Unanimous solutions will haunt all parties in the future. This approach uses the win/win model of negotiations. Because the participants are tied together, this style is a good choice.

Collaboration is often used by the collaborator to brainstorm and solve problems. Participants will view themselves as being on the same side. They will often form groups of people from both companies to develop proposals that are feasible for them both. It is possible that there will not be one side of the negotiation table, but instead a mixture of teams sitting around a circle table.

Any one of the above styles could lead to positive negotiations. Let's find out which set is the best for which style.

The Dominator: This can work in business when there is a weak opponent who can be intimidated and forced into an agreement. It would be better if this person didn't come back to you again. This style is the style for the authoritarian. It is all about control and power.

This is a vicious cycle that will lead to more resentment if you keep dealing with it for a long time. This approach might work if I am dealing directly with an organization/person I will not deal with again. I'm thinking of buying a home. I want a fantastic deal. I win, they fall-I'm fine with that. You go to get a car. You won't be buying again from this seller or this lot. This may work well for you.

If you're the Dominator, everything is about you. Your actions are rationalized so that, if I get the deal done, I'm happy. It is not my problem if it does not work for the other party.

This will not work if you deal daily with these people and this business.

The Retreater-The Retreater won't tolerate confrontation or strong discord, but he doesn't want to be in a relationship. They stick to their established procedures and practices. It is hard to believe that if we have done this before, it will be the same again. It can be hard to get them out from their comfort zone. This strategy could be a good fit for you if your only goal is to stay safe. Retreaters love deals that are similar in nature to their earlier deals.

It may not be good for you long-term. Also, it may make it hard to get loyalty from another party. But, in a certain case, it might work. This loyalty issue is very important. Let's take a look at this. Because of the lack of personal contact over the years, we never got to know each other. An offer comes in from another vendor, offering a deal that is slightly better than the one we had with your company. It is a better offer. They are extremely likable. The picture is clear. I am compelled to jump to the new seller.

This is because I am a person who struggles to relate to people with my personality. I'm able to be dominant but also adapt and can sometimes accommodate others. But, I tend to be collaborative. These are the styles I use often. I have never retreated in my entire life. That is almost impossible with my outgoing personality.

The Accommodator-The Agcommodator enjoys harmony. To achieve harmony, they are always open to concessions and "meet the middle." This style works well for many aspects in your personal or business life. Accommodators respect people and value relationships. There is nothing negative to say about this. Accommodators are my biggest concern. They can get "lost" in the agreement and forget their "bottom lines," while trying to please each side. They forget what it is they must achieve from these negotiations. I fear they will "give up the store". They will consider a compromise in every area of the agreement. If there is an objection they will search for a solution. Sometimes, it may be impossible to find an accommodating way to negotiate if you require something very specific.

The Collaborator - A Collaborator finds a way to make a deal work for both of them. This approach focuses on the acknowledgment of the needs and desires of the other party. By virtue of their problem-solving mindset, collaboration is results-oriented. This style builds rapport and respect quickly, as it is problem-solving. So why not make this your go-to style? You should always remember that your style will reflect the situation. If you need to "roll" the opposing side or are in a hurry, you may not want to employ a collaborative style.

All is fair in negotiation and war, as experienced negotiators will confirm. Dominators have a win/lose attitude. How long do you expect to take to convince the other side to adopt a collaborative approach? You can adjust your style according to the circumstances.

Chapter 4: What Makes Negotiation Possible?

This is possible by using key concepts from both integrative or distributive negotiation methods. Every party has their 'bottom line' or reservation. It is a threshold beyond which a party will not accept or go, and it should be reached before negotiations can end. Raiffa suggests that the value should be kept private as it is something that other participants are not aware of. The bottom line helps frame the possibilities and the scope of an agreement. You can take this example:

Reservation points overlap: A sweet deal

A local milk producer and chief milk supplier are currently negotiating a contract. Although the producer may be willing to pay less than the maximum price for the product, she is fully aware of the fact that the purchase will still be worth the 10le/liter. Here, the producer holds a reservation at 10le/liter. The supplier is aware that the producer wants a higher price, but he hopes negotiations will bring him a better deal. Accordingly to him, he would sell his raw dairy milk to the manufacturer at a minimum of 10le/liter. This is his initial price, since he won't accept any deal below it.

The Basics Of Effective Negotiation Strategies

Negotiation occurs most often in legal proceedings. Negotiation theory is a common study for professional negotiators. This involves various partnerships with brokers, legislators and diplomats, as well multinational company owners.

Negotiating Tactics

There are many methods of categorizing basic elements in negotiation. Three elements cover the basics of negotiation: substance, procedure and behavior. These elements are dependent on the parties involved. The process refers to how one side negotiates with the other. Substance and behavior, on the other hand, are related to the relationship between two people and the outcome of their negotiations.

There are also basic elements to negotiation: process, strategy and tools.

An Overview of Negotiation Approaches

Theorists have different views on the question of classifying the leading school in negotiations theory. Daniel Druckman explains that the most influential schools of theory in negotiation theory are those who adhere to four methods to negotiation. Negotiation is defined as: diplomatic politics and puzzle solving, organizational management, negotiation, and a game of bargaining. On the other hand, Howard Raiffa suggests a number of 'approaches' designed around the scopes of prescription-description and symmetry-asymmetry.

This overview of negotiation methods or schools of thought is based in part on William Zartman's summary. Zartman is a researcher and theorist on negotiations. It comprises five main approaches or levels. They include the structural, the processual (commonly known as 'concession-exchange), the strategic, the integrative, and the behavioral approaches.

Structural methods

These approaches see negotiated results as the result of specific structural features or characteristics. These features might include characteristics such as the composition, whether each side is comprised of different groups or monolithic, or the relative strength and issues of the rival parties. These approaches can provide insight into the patterns of relations and objectives between the parties.

Analysts tend to refer to negotiations as engagement scenarios that involve rivals with conflicting goals. Analysts who adopt a structural method in their studies tend to place emphasis upon the resources available for a negotiation.

However, structural methods have some limitations. Critics argue that structural explanations are too focused on power and the most difficult aspects. A structural approach emphasizes taking positions. It is important for negotiators to realize that blind attachment to a negotiation regardless of its outcome can cause a failure in the long-term strategy.

Strategic approach

Strategic approaches draw from mathematics, rational choices theory, and decision analysis. The structural approach focuses on the functions of means (like the power in negotiations), while strategic models are focused on the end parts of ends (objectives). These models are also rational decision-making. Negotiators are known as rational choice-makers with identified substitutes. They make decisions based upon their evaluation of the option which will maximize their gains, also known as 'payoffs. Actors select from a selection of possible actions to help them achieve their goals. Every actor has an extraordinary 'incentive system'. It consists of a range cost-related to diverse actions combined with a range potential prospects that reveal the livelihoods and results of various actions.

These approaches can be considered normative. Because they are rooted on the belief that there is an ultimate solution for all negotiation difficulties, they seek to symbolize "what ultrasmart super-humans should be doing in competitive, interactive settings such as bargains." As they search for the "best answers" in every negotiation. This is called Symmetrically Scriptive. These strategic approaches form the basis of negotiation models like critical-risk theory and game theory.

Game theory: It is based on mathematical models that predict, forecast, or recommend the actions that parties should take to maximize their individual benefits. Each actor's choices will determine the outcome of any given choice.

Ellsberg presents a critical risk model to crisis bargaining. This is similar in concept to game theory. It uses basic utility numbers, which help to understand decision-making. This model assumes that parties use probability estimates to determine whether they should concede or not, and how to negotiate in a disaster situation.

Behavioral approach

It emphasizes the individual characteristics and personalities of negotiators in determining the result and how they will be negotiated.

Behavioral models might describe negotiations as interactions among personalities that take different forms such as headliners or softliners or warriors or shopkeepers. Here, negotiators could be depicted as either diplomatically allowing the other party to continue peace or fighting for justice.

This approach is rooted in psychological and experimental traditions, but also centuries-old diplomatic deals. These traditions believe that negotiations are about individuals, not employers, unions or nations. The game theory is based on the assumption that the parties to a negotiation game' are uniformly rational and payoff maximizing. The behavioral approach emphasizes human skills, emotions, tendencies, and tendencies. They might also point out the roles played in the negotiation results by the arts' of personality perception, persuasion and individual motivation. Others have highlighted expectations, relationships. Skills, trust. Culture.

Concession exchange (Processual) approach

This approach shares characteristics of both a strategy approach (results), as well as a structural approach. But they also define a form of mechanism that is more focused on learning. Zartman believes that negotiation can be described as a learning process. In this view (processual approach), parties learn from each other and respond to their concessions. In this view, negotiation is a series or concessions that marks each stage of the negotiation. Both parties used them as a way to convey their intentions, and to motivate others to take action in their place. Both parties "utilize these bids to respond to the earlier counteroffer" and to impact on the subsequent offer; these offers can be a exercise in power.

There is the risk that concession-trading parties may not recognize potential benefits to their mutual dilemmas and instead engage in a negative process that leaves them with fewer gains than if a more creative strategy was chosen.

Integrative Approach

These views are sharply opposed to distributive perspectives that see negotiations as relations that can lead to win-win outcomes. A zero-sum vision of the negotiation's objective is to get one's "limited amount" of pie. However, these integrative strategies and theories are focused on ways to 'expand' the pie or create value to ensure that there is enough for all parties to enjoy the benefits of the negotiation. These strategies and theories use objective criteria to seek out conditions that promote mutual gains and encourage group problem-solving. Integrative approaches are based on cooperation, mutual gain, problem solving and joint decision-making. They encourage all parties to cooperate to find win-win strategies. This means that parties must search for common goals, identify interests, and generate options.

Negotiators may try to build value and create common values. This will help them to decide how and when outputs should be claimed. This approach to negotiations relies on social decision-making as well as political theory, research on labor dispute and international relations.

Negotiating styles

R.G Shell a selfhelp expert has identified these five negotiating types in his latest study. Each style differs depending on the context and the interests of the parties.

- Compromising: This is where individuals or groups try to negotiate deals that are fair or equal for all of the parties. When time is limited, compromisers are useful.

- Competing: This is where people are willing to compete in order to get something. Competitive negotiators possess the strongest instincts to negotiate in almost all aspects. On the flip side, they are often unaware of the importance for "party-based", relationships.

- Collaboration – This refers to individuals who are open to collaborating, and enjoy solving difficult problems in creative ways.

- Collaborators, contrary to other competitors, are skilled at understanding the concerns or interests of parties.

Avoiding – This refers to people who are not interested in negotiations or simply don't like them being negotiated unless necessary.

Avoiders tend to dodge the provoking side of negotiation and are often perceived by others as subtle and tactful.

- Accommodating- These are people who have a history of solving problems for others. Accommodators must be sensitive towards the emotional and verbal states, body language, and emotions of other parties.

Types and types of negotiations

Business negotiation: This is a type of negotiation where the focus is on the provision of a service or product and the desire to satisfy. The contract is commercial, and can be used in a purchase contract (lease, partnership, etc.). (), a command or a convention, an act, or modify certain clauses of price ranges, quality or transport conditions, delivery, etc.

Distributive negotiation - this is a type or negotiation where one of the parties can choose to win or lose. It requires a transaction form that allows one party to win while the other has to lose. At the expense of the grantor, each partner must give their approval.

Negotiation brings opposing interest parties together and turns into a conflict of foresight where one side can win. A consent sign is perceived as weakness. An effective attack is power. The goal of negotiation(s), however, is an arrangement that doesn't consider other parties' interests. In fact it will be better to have the consequence strike hardest.

Integrative Negotiations (win/win) are negotiations that are inclusive if both parties' interest and aspirations will be respected regardless of their origin. It is built around mutual respect and tolerance for differing opinions and objective.

This method of negotiation results in better, more practical solutions. Both parties feel better and their relationships improve. Both sides agree to the solutions and both sides win. This negotiation strengthens and saves money over time.

The negotiation's optic evades conflict situations. Once reached, the negotiation atmosphere is one of optimism as well as confidence. It's easy to appreciate the arrangement. Specific tactics are built upon sharing concessions (e.g. shorter terms of delivery to get an immediate payment).

Rational negotiations - This type of negotiation doesn't allow the parties to have one objective or to obtain their consent. It allows them to work together to find a neutral solution to any differences. To reach this goal, there should be clearly defined shared goals and transparent sincerity without resort to suspicion or concealment.

It starts with the identification of the problems and solutions. Questions such as "How can I display it?" are also addressed. What's wrong? What are the contradicting facts of the situation Where is the evil? It starts with a situation evaluation, focusing in particular on the problem and possible solutions. Next, we discuss and agree on the best ways to solve the problem.

Chapter 5: How To Negotiate A Buyer

Your success as a seller is dependent on your ability and skill to close deals. Negotiating with a buyer becomes even more difficult when you have to meet certain quotas.

19. Exploit a buyer's senses

Visuals are key. You must use all of the senses your customer has. If you bring the experience to a new level, it will guarantee you win a deal. When selling cars, don't just state facts and figures.

Don't just show the vehicle to the customer. Make sure they are able to sit in it. The customer should feel the engine rev. You can open the sound system and let the customer hear the car rev. The leather seats should be smelled. The customer will be able to convince themselves even after a few more days.

20. Make use of the power and persistence

Consistency may not work but persistence is likely to. Salespeople adhere to one golden rule in selling: A prospect customer remains a prospective client until he/she is moved. While that customer remains at your premises you can continue to use all of your magic words with personal charm.

But, to sell a product or service successfully, you need to persevere. Customers might buy whatever they want to in order to reward their over-attention, regardless of whether the intention is positive or negative.

21. Present first, Compare next

It's not possible to say, "We have all the best models of masticating juicers in town," without actually presenting what is actually available. It is certainly a compelling statement. But, avid buyers who are aware that there are many places to buy products from will find it suspicious.

Smart buyers know that it's not just about the offer. The quality of the product being sold as well as the service provided by the retailer is important. Customers shop at trusted stores not just for the best price, but also because they feel safe and are assured a great service.

Comparing yourself with your competitors might make a customer think that you have something hidden, maybe a substandard product that's both cheaper and less quality.

22. Show kindness

Many store salesmen and women don't inform their customers about ongoing discounts, free-item promotionals, and other perks. This is to maintain leverage when negotiating for a deal by using "pay more, get more". Instead of giving full discounts and free items right away, they give so-called freebies to each customer one at a while to create the illusion that they are generous. But they are not generous since the freebies they give are intended to be included in the product. It is only the impression that counts.

Avoid flipping all of your cards simultaneously. Let the impression develop slowly but surely. It is not enough to be generous.

23. In the event of a price increase, send a memo or written notice.

It can't be avoided that prices do fluctuate from time to other. Customers will often dismiss a popular product whose price has been lower over time as a reason for not buying it. Your customers may want to consider checking other stores before they decide to abandon your store. If customers find out that every store has the exact same price hike, it is too late. There will be no reason to offer your services again if other stores are offering the same prices.

Show proof as soon as you notice that the price is going up. This is why so many stores display price increases notices.

24. A big smile is a great way to show your appreciation.

If you want to convince honest customers, nothing is better than a big, genuine smile. Sometimes there's no need for you to complicate. Customers want to buy things and are willing to spend the money. If the prices for each store are the same, it will not matter how sincere you are.

25. Offer post-services

Customers often fear losing what they bought. One does not want to buy a device that is prone to glitches after only a week.

Offer security by providing guaranteed assistance and post-services.

Chapter 6: Negotiation Techniques

Separate The People from The Problem

When you negotiate, you must be able to discern between the issues of people and the more substantive ones.

The negotiation process is influenced by your perceptions and emotions. Personal perceptions can make it difficult to focus on the topic of negotiations. This can result in reactions and counterreactions from all the parties. The involved parties will then begin to interpret statements wrongly. You could make a statement that identifies a problem. The other party might interpret it as an attack. These are the key points you need to distinguish between the two.

A good relationship of negotiation is essential

This principle is necessary to negotiate and resolve conflict. Avoid direct confrontation which could lead to anger and fight in negotiations. Create a friendly and relaxed atmosphere in your negotiation. Keep your enemies out of the room. This will make negotiations easier.

Change your Perception

Every person in the negotiations room sees the conflict differently. In reality, the conflict lies in each party's perception of the problem. It is crucial to get to know and accept the different opinions on the issue.

A negotiator's most important skill is the ability see the situation from the perspective of the other side. This doesn't necessarily mean that you should agree with each other, but it will help to create a solid foundation for your negotiations. You will know what the other side needs and want.

This is a way to address these differing perceptions.

Know and feel your emotions

Understanding and recognizing the emotions of both the other person and yours is another way to help you separate people from the problem. First, understand your emotions. You need to understand what makes you angry about the problems you are trying solving and who you believe is responsible. Next, assess your emotion and then get to know the emotions of your counterparts. Negotiating becomes easier when you and the counterparts acknowledge your emotions.

Allowing the other side to express their feelings is the best way for them to deal with it. Give them the chance to express their feelings. Just listen and not respond. Don't respond to emotions. They may also abuse you, or falsely accuse. Don't interrupt the conversation or try to defend them. You should remain calm and pay close attention to what the other person is saying. They will feel more comfortable expressing themselves once they have calmed down.

You can show your concentration by using symbolic gestures, such as nodding the head. You'll be able to show that you care about them and understand their feelings. This gesture can be used as a form if apology. It can also defuse their emotions. Even if your actions are not directly related to you, use gestures. You'll have the upper hand during negotiations if you do all of these things.

Concentrate on Interests, not Positions

Normally, when you enter into a negotiation you have your own interests. The interests of the other party in the negotiation are also important. Therefore, the interest of all those involved in the negotiations will define the problem. As you negotiate identify the interests of your counterparts. It is possible to negotiate when you have a clear understanding of your counterparts' interests.

Try looking for hidden interests in the positions that your counterparts are holding on to. By asking yourself questions, you can find out why. Why does this party still hold that position? What is the point of this party's stance? Why are they refusing to take the action that I suggested? These questions will give an insight into other parties' interests, which will enable you to negotiate with them one step more effectively. It is important to identify conflicting interests for both sides. You can discuss these with your counterparts and see if you can come to an agreement. Next, identify your common interests.

Each side has its multiple interests. It's impossible to please all sides. Instead, prioritize your own interests. Make the other side recognize how legitimate and valuable your interests. You should be precise and straight to the point when addressing them. Make sure they know you are serious and interested in their concerns.

Accept their feelings and concerns as part the problem. Show them that they are understood and that you are ready to help them. You can highlight the common interests of both sides and negotiate a deal. Be open to ideas that balance the interests of both parties.

"I am only asking for fairness" strategy

This is an easy strategy, but very effective when you're negotiating in a business setting. This implies that you will only accept the current market prices or industry standards for your requests. It relieves your obligation to justify any action in your negotiations. Once you insist that you do not want to negotiate for the standard, it is up to your side to convince you otherwise.

Mutual Gain by Inventing Options

In order for a negotiation to go forward and be successful, everyone involved must benefit. To achieve mutual gain, you need to make sure that there is room.

Some obstacles can prevent the invention and development of options.

Premature judgement

Don't judge other sides based only on your interests. Sometimes, you may believe that everyone wants to win in the negotiation. This can lead to defensiveness, and you won't be able build a relationship of mutual benefit.

You should see your partner as not your enemies but as friends with differing interests.

Searching for a single answer

It is unlikely that you will get the right answer for every problem that involves more parties. Avoid wasting your time trying for the right solution. These problems can arise from many different causes. You only need the solution to the problem, not the cause. When you negotiate, make sure to consider mutual gains.

Think that solving the problem should be the responsibility of the other side

This is a common misconception that will prevent you from being successful in negotiations. You don't have to be completely responsible for the problems that your counterpart faces. Each party is responsible for the problem in some fashion. You cannot blame one side. Each side must contribute to the solution. It doesn't matter if you think your counterpart is the cause of the problem. This will make negotiations more difficult and take longer to reach an accord.

Here are some steps to help with your inventions:

*Define the problem

You need to be able to understand the problem. All parties need to understand the problem. This is the first thing that you need to do in order to come up with mutually beneficial solutions.

* Analyze the problem

Together, you can determine the causes of the problem. It is important to identify the root cause and not blame others. Avoid wasting time on this topic, as it could distract you from the topic of negotiations.

*Come up to Approaches

You should look for ways to address the problem. Identify potential solutions to the problem and what you can do to benefit from them. Don't be specific on any side at this point, just give your thoughts.

*Action ideas

Take the time to identify the steps you should take. Next, assign each team a specific task. This will ensure that each side is able to contribute to the solution.

Now you can begin inventing innovative options for mutual advantage with that preparation. Inventing ideas is different from judging them. You won't be able to create new inventions if you start judging them. Let everyone know that you are attempting to invent options that will benefit both parties.

Brainstorming is the best method to use here. Discuss the main purpose of the negotiation. Anyone would like to win the negotiation. Select a few people for a particular task. You can choose either to follow a set order or go wild. You should ensure that everyone is present during this session. If necessary, make sure to establish rules.

After brainstorming you can start analysing the ideas that you have generated. The first step to identifying the most promising ideas is to analyze them. Talk about these ideas with your colleagues and work together to improve the product. It is better to take each idea and evaluate it one at a while, then decide based on what you see.

Professionals are better if you are involved in huge negotiations that could affect the stability of countries or other countries. Take the time to get the opinion of professionals and review them. Invent agreements that reflect your strengths and allow your counterparts to choose the best. Find common gains and interests in the agreements. These interests will give you the best opportunities. For an agreement to be reached, it is necessary to consider options that appeal both to one and the other. All parties must benefit from the decisions that are made. Consider their interests to make this happen.

*Remember to use objective criteria

Most negotiations end in failure because the delegates divert from their main objective. It is much easier to deviate than to remain focused on the main objective of the negotiations. It is important to keep your discussion focused on the main topic. Avoid emotional attachments and personal interests.

It is important that the objective criteria used be independent of any side's will. This is where you get the procedure for resolving the dispute. These criteria should be followed by the person asking the question.

These objective criteria should be available to both sides and not favoritism.

Alternatives

Every coin has 2 sides. To avoid losing your plan A, have a plan for B.

This will require brainstorming as well as thorough investigation of all viewpoints.

Your Best Alternative To Negotiation Agreement should be prepared. You will need to decide whether to proceed with alternative arrangements that are reached by negotiation or with the end of the negotiation. Be sure to consider the BATNA of your opponent. A list of actions is a must in order to make a good BATNA. These ideas can be improved and used to create practical alternatives. The best alternatives are those that appeal to your interests. Remember that a good BATNA will be based on you interests. It will be easier to negotiate if your interests are understood.

While we may be able to see the many strategies involved in negotiation, communication is vital.

Three issues can occur during communication. One, you and the other negotiators are not speaking to each another. One party might not be hearing you properly or may have a misunderstanding.

You might look for the following solutions in this scenario:

Listen actively

Being attentive will allow you to hear what the other side has in common and what is troubling them. It will project a positive outlook about yourself. The other side will also see your willingness and ability to reach a solution.

Recognize and acknowledge the viewpoints of others

As this will cause heated debate, don't try to oppose them. Don't forget that acknowledgement isn't agreement. Recognizing the grievances of others is a sign that you are committed to the negotiation process.

Talk-don't debate

You don't need to attack others when you have an opportunity to speak. Instead, be clear about your objectives. If you are interrupted, don't hesitate to stop the discussion.

Talk about yourself only

Be open about your feelings, goals, and expectations. They are not your priority. Remember that the reason they aren't there is the deal you want.

So what happens if negotiations don't produce an outcome? Let's see how to get out of a stalemate and make it win-win.

Stalemate in negotiations

This happens when neither party wins or loses in a negotiation. You'll find yourself back at where you started. This can happen when one side focuses on its own interests and ignores the needs of the other. It could also happen if one side is aggressively defending its position, and the opposing side is doing the same.

All parties must support a win/win outcome for negotiation to be successful. All parties can move forward with their needs being met if they agree to this outcome. It improves trust between the parties involved, and everyone is satisfied. Here are the steps to achieve a win/win outcome.

Your negotiation scope should be expanded

Avoid limiting your negotiation to one issue. If you do that, you will only have one winner. If you are negotiating for the price on a certain commodity, there are other factors that can be considered. You may include factors such as delivery fees, quality and supplementary goods, or services.

Remember that the needs and wants of the other person are different

The other side has goals that may differ from yours. This is something you need to accept. Even though you might think it is a fair price, the other person may disagree. Understanding the differences in your perceptions and needs will help you find a win-win situation.

Do not assume you can understand the needs of another party

You can't know what your counterparts think. Don't assume your counterparts want this or that. Ask them what you want. Don't be afraid to ask them questions if they aren't happy with you. Your relationships with your counterparts should be improved.

Chapter 7: Negotiating For Your Benefit

Negotiation must be done before any business agreement can be signed. For any business deal or agreement to be reached, all parties must come together at the table. Each party sits down with the common goal to reach a contract. But, what the details of that contract are depends on the negotiation. This skill can be learned by practicing simple negotiation strategies. Some people may have the wildest negotiation tips, such providing others with caffeine and then allowing them to make decisions under a controlled drug-induced state. These and many other such tricks are too devious. You need to be careful and trust yourself enough to refrain from trying them. These devious negotiating techniques are not only dangerous and evil, they can also backfire. Here are some strategies you can use on the negotiation table to get a yes for your new venture or deal.

Parts and Negotiation

Negotiations can often fall apart because parties are too rigid or adopt an "all of the above" approach. This leads to unsuccessful negotiations. Dealing in smaller sections is the best strategy when you are at the negotiating table. Instead of fighting over one huge war, instead deal with individual disagreements to reach a consensus. This is how you can move ahead.

The Fair and Square Approach

This strategy involves claiming that whatever your position is, it is only fair based upon industry standards. However, the other side must convince the other to agree to concessions. You can negotiate your way to success by simply asking for what's fair.

The Four Principles to Yes

As I mentioned earlier, there are four key principles to successful negotiation. These are key ways to get a positive response and allow you to move forward with the negotiations. These principles include seperating from the problem and emotion, investigating the real concern, focusing on your own interest, creating new options, or alternatives, and remaining objective through the use of principles fairness.

Take Control

This strategy allows you complete control over all aspects of negotiation. You will have complete control of the agenda. This gives you confidence as well as the ability to make decisions. If you have full control of the agenda, you can decide which topics should be addressed.

The "Offer Concessions" tactic

You want to ensure that your negotiations are successful. In business, it is beneficial for both sides to meet others halfway. Never reveal your interests or bottom line in negotiations. Only after you give the other side the benefit-of-the doubt that they have reached a good agreement can you negotiate.

Ask questions rather than ask

If the other person isn't willing to negotiate on certain points or makes a clear line, ask him/her why. Ask questions to keep the conversation going. Rigidity is a recipe for arguments and disagreements that are very difficult solutions. It is important to ask why the No was given and not just follow the example of the other party. Ask the question and then you can offer your answer.

Find your points of convergence and make a positive note.

This strategy can be used in a number of ways, such as "You're wrong about that" and "I agree". These terms encourage collaboration, which is crucial to keeping the other person satisfied. Many business meetings may be spread over several meetings. Make sure you leave each meeting positive and encouraging. This will make the other person feel more comfortable and open to a possible agreement.

Do Your Research

Research and information will never fail you. The party with more information will always be better and will have more influence. More leverage will result in more bargaining chips. You know what they don't know, and so you can offer them more. Be sure to do your research and impress them. It is possible to direct negotiation towards your benefit by impressing other parties who are willing and interested in a deal. Sometimes, sharing a few details about the other party can improve collaboration. Knowing all details about the other business is crucial to your success in a business relationship.

Ultimatums: Get the Deal

Sometimes, it is okay not to comply with ultimatums. Or to help your business grow. Sometimes, it is acceptable to accept an offer from another party if they are the only vendor/option left for you business. It is important to not compromise your business integrity.

Facts over Feelings

Emotions and feelings do not play any role in negotiations that are successful. In fact, they are kept out of the negotiation process. Emotions are not good for the negotiation process and can make it difficult. It's better than using emotions to get a point across, rather than bad behavior or anger. Avoid any behavior that may make it look like you are only interested in negotiating a deal. While this may be true, it is not necessary to use terms such as "I believe", and "I hope", etc. It's possible to express a collective feeling by using "us"/"we", which conveys that everyone is involved with the decision-making process.

With these strategies in place, negotiations can be made much easier. All you have to do is play the cards correctly, use these strategies, and remain cool. The rest will happen on the table and will definitely be a win,

Chapter 8: The Process Of Negotiation

You could categorize negotiation into several groups depending on how it ends or what the situation is. Let's briefly examine these categories. Later, we will look at the tactics used during negotiations and some effective ways to counter those tactics.

A used car dealer intends to sell one low-end car. The customer and the dealer are both happy if the vehicle is sold for $1000. The dealer loses money, while the customer is able to get a better deal if the car's price falls below $1000. You might be wondering why the dealer would agree to a deal that doesn't benefit him. Let's imagine that the dealer runs out of space. If he had better cars, those cars would be more expensive than the current display car. To accommodate more lucrative deals, the dealer might sell the first vehicle for a slightly higher price.

In another example, if the car is sold for over $1000, the buyer loses money since he paid less. This can happen due to inaccurate or incomplete information. The buyer might have noticed something extraordinary with the seller's care. In the last scenario, both the customer and seller failed to reach a common understanding. Thus, the sale failed. Both of these situations were not beneficial for either party.

Collaborative tactics

These are all common strategies used in negotiations to find a resolution. These types of negotiations aim to reach a win/win outcome. It is almost impossible to achieve a Win/Win situation where both sides win. There are however ways to compensate for the losses of the other party, such as tradeoffs or other strategies. You can take advantage of coupons and discounts offered by retailers or airlines. After being presented with an offer of trade-offs, it is crucial that the participant fully understands and evaluates the offer before signing up. Another popular tactic to use is the trial balloon, in which one party makes hypothetical proposals to the other to gauge their reactions. These offers will be included in sentences that start with "what is if" and/or "suppose." You can calmly explore the offer if it is being made. During the discussion, you should clarify the amount of commitment and value.

Neutral tactics

Another common set of techniques used in negotiations is this. These common methods are frequently used in negotiation. Participants in this negotiation do not try to beat each other. The goal of these negotiations is to achieve the desired results. Negotiators are known to use many tactics, including the drawing of deadlines. This is to ensure that the activity discussed can be completed in the given time. If you receive such an offer, you may try to understand the reason behind it. If you are not comfortable with the offer, you might insist that the other person focus on its value and the solution, rather than the time.

In such negotiations, you should also locate the people who are asking for the presence of higher officials without any direct stake. These requests could be understood depending on the requirements. If you are not convinced that you have the need for a third person, you might express your dissatisfaction. Other administrative constraints such as budget issues can be cited here. Before you make any comments about these issues, it is essential to understand and analyze them.

Manipulative techniques

One group may resort to manipulative strategies for their selfish gains. A skilled negotiator needs to be able to recognize such tactics and create countermeasures. Future promises are one example of this manipulative tactic. They might make future promises in return for your concessions. Under this condition, the negotiator might ask for documentations to confirm any future promise. In order to return favors, the other side could be required to sign contracts.

Threats are another way of putting pressure on the participants. One reminds each other of the importance and fairness of a process that leads to a common goal. It is impossible for them to do so without their cooperation.

Exposing competitor information such as prices offered by other parties or any similar information is another manipulative tactic. This issue will be resolved if you are prepared.

There is no need for every negotiation to be structured in the same way. However, this outline shows how an ideal structure should be used to ensure a smooth and successful negotiation. Four phases represent each stage of a negotiation for your convenience.

Phase 1

Negotiation requires preparation, just like every other activity. This is where the real work begins. You must ensure that everything went according to plan. If you are having problems or things don't work out the way you planned, it is time to reevaluate whether you should continue with negotiations.

Get to know your counterpart. Talk to your counterpart, get to know them and exchange a few pleasant words. To set the stage for the negotiation, you can talk about the things that are important to both parties to help them understand your role in the process. This could be just a sentence, or even a word. It doesn't mean that you have to make it sound like an official staff meeting. The next step is to discuss the agenda with your counterpart. Be clear about the negotiation's scope and outline the boundaries for discussion. Then, set out the rules and guidelines for the session. Check that both sides have reached an agreement on these matters. You must ensure that these things are in place before you enter into the discussion.

Phase testing

Get to know the points of view of the other side on the common issues. You can then evaluate the merits and draw comparisons with your plans. Try to find any weaknesses in their arguments. Be polite and gentle in your arguments. Also, try to figure out their limits.

Moment phase

This is where you will find the bargaining aspect of the negotiation. Send them your offers and watch their reactions. This exercise will help you both to solve the problem. After you have completed the initial part, you can begin to create a list that includes solutions and recommendations. Then you will need to add your contributions and responsibilities. This is the main idea behind negotiation. To create a mutually-accommodating plan, it is necessary to spend time.

Concluding phase

You can decide on your actions and desired results, based upon the plan that you created earlier. During this phase you can establish terms for cooperation such as the frequency of reviews, time limit, and so forth. It is best to have all of these items together when you have a clear understanding of what is expected.

Chapter 9: Presenting A Case

You will have to present your case. Timing matters, so be patient and pick wisely. You've probably established your credibility and instilled confidence. You will have a good understanding of opposing views, as well as the strengths and weaknesses of their cases. You will also know who is fully behind each opinion and who are against it. There will naturally be some who are against it, and you should now be able to convince them in your favor.

First, make sure you know all details of your case. Even the most important ones. Never think that just because something is true, it means that every aspect of your case is perfect. Being aware of your weaknesses will make it easier for you to defend them. Be prepared to counter arguments and ask diversionary queries that will help you keep your eyes on the weak points in the opposing view.

Present your case clearly and calmly. Have the patience to listen to others who may question your position. It is important to demonstrate that you have listened when the other side argues. Use inclusive expressions, such as "we and us" as opposed to "you and them". If there are people you know who agree with your position, invite them to speak up. This is your presentation. Be prepared to deliver it.

Once you have clearly stated all points you want to promote, give a short summary of each argument. Focus on the weaknesses of the other position and your strengths. While you should display passion about the case you are presenting then don't let that passion lead you to anger or lose control.

Being able to explain clearly is one of your most valuable tools for convincing others. This is a powerful weapon that you can learn and practice. You should improve your oral skills. By making sure that you speak clearly in every conversation you engage in, you will be able to make a powerful tool out of it.

Chapter 10: Characteristics Of Negotiation

Negotiation is a communication and persuasion process between individuals, parties, or groups that have diverse interests to achieve desired goals.

The first step in the negotiation process is to determine if there are any differences between the opinions or objectives of the 2 sides.

All parties involved in negotiations will communicate and cooperate to achieve their objectives.

Negotiating involves both the parties trying to find a mutually profitable position. They do this by trying to influence and influence each other. Both sides believe that negotiations will lead to the desired outcomes or at minimum acceptable results for all. Negotiation can be described as the collaboration of two parties or groups over a common decision regarding certain issues.

There are always ways to improve communication skills in the negotiation process.

Your role as negotiator is to help people understand and come to mutually beneficial agreements.

A better understanding of people helps them understand their wants and needs. These people are often embarrassed to hear that they aren't good at negotiation, communication or managing conflict.

If you feel that someone does not have the right skills, it is your job to pull them and help them to improve their communication and negotiation skills. Because the person will only be open to you if he/she is comfortable and not antagonized, it is important that you are able to show tactfulness. You will need to be sensitive and flexible depending on what type of personality you are dealing.

Take care not to be shy in asking questions about your counterparts as part of negotiations. If you feel the urge to clarify any matter, do not hesitate to do so. This is because words can take on different meanings depending upon their context. Even if the meanings of words are identical, it's important to clarify when in doubt. These are called relative words. This is why it is so important to understand relativity in negotiation.

Also, relative words could be defined as descriptive and nonspecific words that are used in connection to other words. Some words in this category are large, often many large and high quality. If you are unsure about the meaning of these words, do not hesitate to ask.

Prepare for negotiations

You need to be prepared for whatever negotiation you're involved in, whether it's personal or professional.

Preparation covers 3 areas.

Clear communication is key to boosting confidence and productivity. At the same, you need to be aware of your strengths as well as weaknesses. You need to know your strengths and weaknesses. For instance, are you patient enough to listen to the other person or do you interrupt between listening and ignoring the message? You must prepare yourself for negotiation by keeping these things in your mind.

It is also important that you know something about the other person before you begin negotiating. This will allow for confidence and enable you to maneuver the negotiation in favor of your side.

If you are going to interview for a job, you will need to do some research on the interviewer (or the company), which can help to establish a stronger connection and give better, more targeted answers. This will increase the likelihood that you will be hired.

You should also be prepared for changes in the market. If you find yourself in a situation where you need to negotiate, do not hesitate to ask for help. Research the subject before you start. Do your research and you will be the smartest person on the table.

Knowledge is power. That knowledge becomes useful in the course and negotiation.

Different negotiation styles

Competitive style

Co-operative approach

A problem-solving style

Tools for successful negotiation

A variety of tools are available to help with negotiation. You can maximize the potential benefits of the situation by selecting the right tool at a suitable time.

You can also use it to control the negotiation process.

Some of these tools can be found here:

Trust - This tool or principle is of vital importance. Without trust, negotiation cannot take place anywhere on earth. It is assumed by all parties that they trust and treat each other during the negotiation process.

Perception - The alignment between your image and the attitude that others see is what you call perception.

This is because the person sitting in front of you will learn more about you by looking at how you act, regardless what you say.

If you don't believe in what you believe, others might not believe.

Strategies and tactics: Using predetermined strategies during negotiation increases your chances to succeed. The right strategies and techniques are essential.

Negotiation involves many steps.

Stage 1 - Assess the problem and decide which strategy will work best to get it solved.

This can be achieved by assessing the options available, your leverage, as well as various approaches to court, arbitration, mediation and facilitation.

Once you have selected a method, move on the next stage.

Stage 2. Communicate with the other party.

This can either be done by mail or phone.

Communicate with them your reason for the deal, your needs and suggest ways to work together.

By building relationships and establishing trust, your value and your proposal are able to expand your network. You will also be able to build your organization's and personal credibility.

Stage 3 - Analyze background information.

This involves gathering data and figures pertinent to the other side.

Before you move ahead, be sure to check the information.

Identify the psychological, procedural or substantive interests of all involved.

Stage 4- Design an effective negotiation plan.

It includes different tactics and strategies that encourage them consider the deal.

It includes ways to deal in different situations or problem areas when you are negotiating.

Stage 5: Building trust & cooperation. This stage is essential for every deal.

Negotiators need to be able use strategies to handle strong emotions like anger and resentment.

It includes the recognition and treatment of any personal or legitimate problems.

Clear communication is essential here.

Stage 6 - Initiating negotiations.

This involves the introduction and acceptance of all parties.

Stage 7- Define issues, set an agenda.

It involves identifying and solving problems for all parties.

Learn more by listening well, asking open-ended question and discussing the issues.

Stage 8- Reveal hidden interests.

It involves identifying individuals' interests at the time that the dispute occurs.

This is done to ensure everyone understands each other's concerns and tries agreeing on a common purpose.

Stage 9- Finding alternative ways to reach amicable arrangements

Resolved issues or the needs.

It is about creating awareness, generating objective standard, brainstorming, using trial and error, generating multiple solution options, looking for win/win solutions, and trading concessions that each party values differently.

Stage 10- Evaluation of settlement options- Considering the possibilities for reaching settlement.

Consider the pros and disadvantages of each choice, assess the interest of all involved, and find alternative ways to achieve those interests.

Stage-11 - This is stage eleven, the most important phase of any negotiation.

For the close of the deal, make substantive agreements and offer incremental concessions.

Stage 12: Formal settlement- It involves the formal contract or memorandum d'accord (written), and monitoring and evaluation processes.

The development of enforcement and commitments systems takes place here.

It takes disciplined focus, preparation and hard work to reach your goals.

To avoid any confusions between your goals, day dreaming, and the goals you have set for yourself, you need to make sure you are not the only one setting them.

Writing a bestseller is a day dream. A goal is to write a book about one subject that can make an important contribution to society.

Set realistic goals to achieve in negotiations.

Building your negotiation process

It is important to keep the following points in mind as you begin negotiations.

Real base

Aspiration base

Deal qualification

Identification of the purpose behind the deal (for yourself or the other person).

Contracting zone

Clarity when defining negotiation & team composition

Negotiation tactics & deal-specific strategies like framing scripts, closing the deal procedures and so on.

Apart from the above factors, you must also find ways to establish a negotiation-conducive environment. This allows negotiators the freedom to work on a daily schedule and without being distracted by unnecessary distractions.

In order to make your negotiation more professional and consistent, you can also create a database. What spiels can you use?

Automation can be improved by using negotiation supporting tools and analysis. This includes the CRM, which is software that is used to run call centers.

Training and coaching higher-level managers to help team members learn best practices in negotiation.

This coaching can also take place on an individual level if necessary.

Set goals & limits

As mentioned, setting your goals requires disciplined concentration and a lot preparation.

If you want to be part of a team, it is also important that you set goals.

It is important to recognize that there are other options available and to have an in-depth understanding of these choices.

Setting limits involves writing them down, establishing your resistance level, sharing knowledge with the team, and not putting yourself in a corner.

You can only achieve success by setting goals.

The best way to set goals is to brainstorm and identify what you truly want. Also, be willing and open-minded to compromise.

It is important to explore all avenues of negotiation.

You can achieve your goals best if you write them down.

Be a good listener

Many people believe that they are good listeners despite not being.

Since your negotiation success is directly related to your listening skills, you should work on improving them. There are many benefits to improving your listening skills.

Here are some tips on how to listen well

Make sure you clear up all mess around your workplace.

Second, count your numbers before you answer any questions or comments.

Third is attentive, even if the other person speaks to you.

Be clear

You must feel confident in the message you are delivering. Congruence means that all your communication (body language, actions, voice) conveys the same message (congruence).

Communication is a key skill in a good negotiator

The best way to communicate your intent or purpose is to be clear and specific.

While conducting the meeting, keep calm

Learn to deal tactfully.

This can be done through constructive contributions to the meetings. Ask questions and get their reactions.

When necessary, intercede, pause or end the conversation.

The ramblers (from your group) can dilute communication and lead boredom and general waste of time.

Use the Pause button to pause.

To keep your emotions in check while you are negotiating, you will need a pause switch.

Some people use their pause button quite often and others not at all.

You can, for instance, use the pause button during heated debates to make sure silence is created if both sides are not on the same page.

It can also be used to help a person calm down and not say anything that could later be regrettable.

If the other person isn't able to think clearly about your offer, in certain situations the absence of the Pause button can be helpful.

Therefore, when negotiating, people shouldn't allow their emotions to drive their actions.

You should stop using your hot keys and instead, use the pause button.

Closing

Despite both parties having agreed to the most important issues, the deal does not always get completed.

There could be many reasons why the same might happen, including being too demanding, being bully or intentionally creating chaos during proceedings.

For people who are in such difficult situations, it is important to take breaks as needed so they can regroup.

Sometimes, disturbances can also be caused by invisible partners.

So, while you are on vacation, take the time to research your opponent's strategy so that you can overcome any obstacles once you return to negotiation.

Sometimes, closing the deal is more complicated than you might think.

Because sometimes, people might not like what you offer. If this happens, it is a good idea to ask more questions and try to solve the problem.

Most of the times, the obstacles you face in closing a deal are not because of anything external. Here, you need to confront your demons and not someone else. You can then take action to remove your fears. This will make it easier to address objections made by others.

Put your ideas into practice

It is important to take initiative in order to achieve your goals.

It is important to follow your plan and perform certain tasks.

This will make it easier to be more efficient.

This is how you create your action plans.

Prioritize goals.

Identifying and completing specific tasks requires you to identify the right actions.

Identify key individuals who can aid you in performing each task.

Identify and overcome obstacles during each step.

Calculating the date for completion of all action plans

All types of negotiations

You can apply the basic negotiation actions to any situation.

Some negotiations are out of reach for these skills. However, you must still concentrate on the basic skills.

Chapter 11: Clever Psychological Buyer/Seller Negotiation Tricks

"In life and business, you don't always get what is due, but you negotiate what you receive."

(Chester L. Karrass)

The field of spying is a fast-paced environment. These skills are crucial for your success. Although I wouldn't call myself a professional salesperson, I do have a great deal of experience in the field. No matter your occupation, you will always sell something. There are times when you have to sell or buy something.

These principles were taught to you by the FBI. These principles are crucial psychological tools to know even if they aren't relevant to sales. After all, you will be involved in the buyer/seller side of things sooner or later.

The Boulwarism Approach

Boulwarism (or bargaining) is a strategy for negotiating that was first developed by General Electric's vice president Lemuel Boulware. It is a result from all the labor law disputes he had to have with the various unions. It's intended to be a final offer.

If you are not ready to be very specific in your approach, it is possible to opt for a more gentle version of the "all that I have" strategy. The strategy's basic idea is to declare that "this all I have" at the beginning of negotiations. It's a fundamental scarcity tactic. The idea is to set a budget which is between 20% and 30% less than the current asking value, and to stick to it. This strategy works best for larger items, such as houses or cars. However, it is equally applicable to smaller items. Setting a maximum price upfront will help sellers set a limit and allow them to make concessions in order to bring the price down. This is especially true in situations where you can invoke empathy and sympathy.

Boulwarism can also be a risky strategy. The final offer you make upfront is not always a good idea. Particularly if the product you are looking to purchase is in high demand, the dealer may just wait for someone who will pay the full price. But if you do your research in advance to identify these conditions, it could be a very profitable approach.

Trial ballooning

This tactic is also known as "trial Closing" in sales. It serves as a starting point. The idea behind this is to begin with the final offer, a tentative one that you thought of. It's up to you to try it and see if it works. Don't be afraid, however, to get big. The first offer you receive in an exchange is usually the worst. While an aggressive offer may 'anchor' the price at a high point, even though the other side will almost always bring you lower from there, you will still be in the better position overall. It's possible that they may take the trial balloon right away, especially if you are trying to find a resolution quickly.

Start with statements like, "If possible, we can reach an agreement on XYZ," but it is much more likely that you will initially be questioned. However, you can now find a way to compromise and come up with a solution that works for both of your interests.

Auction Model

This strategy is only viable if there are several buyers. It is simply the act that you play one buyer against another in order create a buying frenzy. This will drive up the selling price.

Humans are competitive creatures by nature. They can be driven to the extremes when they face opposition to what they desire. The instinctive need to possess something is almost a given, even though we may not have rationally weighed the actual use for it. It makes bidding wars exponentially more likely.

I witnessed a deal between two prominent African dictators once. While they had initially been there for their own business, they decided to come together in order to purchase more state-ofthe-art weaponry that would increase their respective arsenals. The broker who set the meeting up, and who was also the biggest arms dealer of the southern half of the hemisphere, asked them to both participate in the same session, as his time was extremely short.

After dictator number 1, had settled his business with some auto firearms, and a few T90 Russian tank tanks, he sat back as the dealer presented the real prize. They were a collection of remote-controlled Reaper Drone's. This was an older version of the MQ9's. They could fly high elevation missions and deliver important payloads, all from a computer screen thousands miles away.

"Eh, why haven't you offered these to me?" the first man shouted in an African accent. Following was a succession of counter offers and offers that were all higher than the first for the set on sale of drones. Although I don't know this for sure but it is almost certain that an arms dealer set up the meeting knowing these two men would enter the bidding fight (for the lack of a better word) that quickly followed.

This is a very dramatic example of an auction-style negotiation in practice. It's also your job in everyday life to bring buyers together when needed, though in a far more amicable setting than the one I've just described. But it is up to them to subtly influence them into this process, and then let them handle it themselves. Let each one be aware and open to the offer of the other, and then let them go.

Offer Biasing

This tactic is great for when you have a variety of options. You can start the discussion by putting forward seemingly neutral and mutual options. However, these options will be heavily or moderately biased in favor of you. The idea behind this is to present a list of options that will make it easier for you to choose from if none is made. Avoid removing anything not of your interest, and instead present a selection that will most naturally lead to the best options for you.

There are natural biases that every person has. The best negotiation strategy is one where you play to them by adding and taking away options as professionally as possible. This tactic doesn't sound so shady or deceitful. The opposing party can always decline or add to their options if they choose. It can be very helpful to know the pros and cons of each option before making a decision. It's similar in that it anchors a set or objectives and sets the price for "All I can".

This technique is often very effective in more relaxed settings with friends and family. It's a good idea to suggest to your friends two movies you want to see. Then, add a third movie that you don't wish to see. You have already set the tone of what everyone will pick. Real estate agents use this strategy when showing prospects properties. They first bring buyers to view two properties. After that, they show them a third more within their budget. The buyers are free to make as many choices as they wish but will be able to see the more expensive houses in their head once they have considered the biased options.

Russian Front

If you have some control of a situation in which you need to negotiate, another decision-based strategy is the "Russian Front" method. It is an expression that dates back to World War II in Nazi Germany. The fighting on the Eastern front was between European Axis powers (Soviet Union) and European Axis. It was one if the most brutal conflict zones of history. In it, you were just about as likely to die from cold as from a Russian shot. There were many reasons why German soldiers loathed it.

This strategy attempts to portray a very dark picture of the original option you are offering. It is one that is clearly unfavorable and will cause the person discomfort. Then, follow that up with another offer, which may be a more attractive one or a different kind of olive branch. If you want to sell someone on a job you wish them to do, you could say something like "I know there positions down in warehouse as the folklift truck hospitalized 2 guys recently but it's fine. You can also reach me at head office.

This happens in all criminal and law-enforcement negotiations and interrogations. The accused suspect will usually be told of harsh treatment and lengthy jail sentences before being offered a plea bargain in exchange for better terms. This is a far more difficult situation than in professional negotiations.

Thought-Pattern Interrupts

I have already written about this principle in books. But, the most important thing you can learn from the CIA is to set baselines and establish standards for behavior in all situations. This allows you more easily identify when something is not right. Negotiation can be no different. The trick is to determine what benchmarks your client has created in their mind, and to see if you are able disrupt this line of thinking.

Although you will have to ask them several baseline questions in order to establish cognitive norms, it is well worth the effort. Ask the person what their ideal outlook is on the negotiations and how they see it progressing. I found that being positive during negotiations made it more likely that the person would agree to give up more. It is up to you, the individual, to alter the standard's outlook if it does not match your objectives.

Car salesmen often ask you what kind of vehicle you'd like to have. He may offer to change your mind if you mention that you like family four-door saloons for their fuel efficiency and ample space for your family. It's like a bait-and-switch for your mind.

This is not to say that the above is false. The more expensive car may actually be a better deal. This is the main point: we constantly make these contrastive comparisons. It is your responsibility to shift these paradigms in favor of negotiating any offer you are offered.

Always offer a selection

Another psychological trick you can use is this one, but this time you will be on the selling side or offering side. Research has shown that offering a range rather than a single number to negotiate a price for something almost always works better than asking for a low figure. Let's say you are selling an apartment to someone and would like $500,000 in return. For the asking price, you can offer between $500,000-$550,000

This is often called a "bolstering offer". One could ask, "Why not offer $550,000?" and let the buyers trade you down to $500,000 naturally. However, it is all about perception. Offering this range upfront will show that you are more reasonable from the beginning and more likely avoid aggressive counter-offers. They will feel more obliged than ever to offer somewhere within this range in return for the perceived fairness, goodwill and respect.

This principle is even more applicable when you are asking someone for something, such as a salary negotiation. If you think that you are worth $80,000/year, you should ask for $80,000-100,000. This shows that you are reasonable and will likely make things more pleasant. You are also upwardly adjusting the value of your boss and, who knows? They may even offer a meeting halfway.

Don't just sell your skills; Sell Your Potential

Let me conclude by sharing a strategy you can use when you need to sell your self. This can be in a job application, relationship, or anywhere else you need to persuade someone to give your ideas a try. Many people spend their time in these kinds of selling situations by focusing on their current accomplishments. These are good things to do. But they're not the ones you should be putting your focus on. Your potential is what you should be focusing on more than anything else.

"The first principle behind contract negotiation does not involve reminding people of past actions; it involves telling them what you intend to do in future."

(Stan Musial)

A Stanford-Harvard Study has found that the person's potential is what attracts others' attention. The potential's uncertainty and ambiguity seems to be more compelling than simply reflecting on facts that are already known and established.

Most people spend all of the time regurgitating past job spec and responsibilities from their resumes. Their future plans are just an afterthought. While I agree that it is beneficial to give specific examples of situations in which you have encountered an issue, or faced a challenge, then explaining the steps taken to overcome them is also a good tactic.

Because almost every white collar job requires critical thinking and problem-solving, employers find these abilities a huge advantage. Machines and AI are making it easier to do repetitive, menial jobs at an alarming pace. I haven't worked a regular position since high school. However, you can easily see the trends from the outside. The next time you try to convince someone of their worthiness, be focused on what they will bring you in the future instead of what they brought you in the present.

Chapter 12: Getting The Groundwork In Place Early

You have done all of your research. Now it is time to go through the application and interview process. This is where you need to be careful. This is how you impress them and make them like you. At the same time, prepare for negotiations. If you're too easy going, it will not be easy to set yourself up for negotiation well. Also, if you focus too much on negotiations, it could discourage them from even considering you. You want them want you!

If you're fortunate enough, you can make it through most of the process without even having to discuss salary. Let's be clear, you don't want to discuss money for as long or as possible. The more you work, the more you can impress your employer. As you get older, your employer will become more invested with you. This makes it more difficult for them to let go. Avoiding salary negotiation is essential. But don't ignore it. This time is an opportunity to market yourself and talk about your value to the company. Through conversation and the end of the interview, ask them questions about the qualities they consider important. You can use this information to help you negotiate and for future interviews. Knowing your success metrics, you can then sell your skills to meet these needs. Give the interviewer reasons to choose you. The interviewer will most likely need to justify the reasoning they give to you so give them plenty to use. This will help you to craft their sales pitch.

Although having an interviewer not mention salary is a great situation, it is not one we can count upon. The application process itself is the most difficult part. It's becoming less common to just submit your resume and complete the application process. There are many questions you'll need to answer. These questions can range from questions about personality to education clarification. These questionnaires might ask you to answer "what salary are you currently earning" or "what salary do your dreams of making?" This questionnaire will ask you two questions. If you are unable to answer them, it is best to leave them blank. As an alternative to "desired income", you might put "Negotiable" in place of "desired". If you need to enter $0 or N/a. Do whatever you can to get over this question. Don't feel guilty, or obligated to provide this number. That's how they want you feel. If you are required to give this number, it is best to do so for both. The mandatory questions or questions that will most likely be asked are those that you have just received. Do not pay, but give what you are paid. Consider the cost of the benefits and perks that you get from your job. Although it may be less likely that the desired salary will be offered, it is still possible. Place the highest end of what you see as your value and what the job at the company pays. You may lose your chance at being selected but it is better that than lowballing yourself, which could cost you thousands of money. This is a dangerous question to make mandatory at this time.

The next obstacle is if an interviewer brings up early pay. Early is a relative term. The worst case scenario is the first interview. If you don't handle it properly, this could lead to awkwardness. A bad interview experience will almost certainly be ruined by awkwardness. The difference between success and failure in this situation is your poker face. Panic spreading across your face as they discuss pay can lead to failure. You must remain confident and firm in every action that you take. Be confident in all actions you take. The worst thing is for them to start the interview by discussing your pay before they can find out whether they like you or if even you are qualified. This is a very classless act. This is very incongruous. It would be just as inappropriate if they asked you about your pay before you sent them your resume. When you are dealing with an individual or company, it is important to keep that in your mind. I want to help you make more money while working at a place where you feel comfortable. Even if they employ you for a lot, they will use shady tactics that will only make things worse. This should be how they treat you. Don't expect things to get worse if it isn't now.

You have been asked this question regardless of your integrity. There are several ways they could ask this same question. We need to be prepared for these different approaches. What are your salary expectations for this position? This is the first question they ask. This can take many forms such as "What's your goal/expectations regarding salary for this position?". However, they will ask you what you WANT to do. This is probably the most commonly asked of both, so let's get to it. Never outright refuse. A simple no will endanger a pleasant conversation you may be having with someone and make you look bad in their eyes. You must be able to control the situation and bring a positive outlook and mutual respect to it. This response can be used to calmly communicate with the interviewer.

"I'm interested and able to find a position that's right for me. I'm confident you will offer a competitive salary on the current market.

If you speak confidently and in a firm voice, it will be clear to them that you are serious. It will also show them that you're serious about the job. Don't delay the interview. This answers shows you are interested in finding a job you love and not just a pay check. This kind of attitude is very attractive to employers. This approach has the added advantage of shaking an interviewer off the topic. It would be awkward for you to press the "pay" button after a similar answer. For successful negotiations, it is crucial that you keep this level playing field.

In the first case, the interviewer wants to find you top number. In the second situation, they will seek to find you lowest number. This is accomplished by asking you what you make. This question can be posed in many different ways. However, the most common one is "What's your current salary?" I used to want to simply ask my coworkers how much they earned to keep it fair. It would do more harm then good so that will remain a personal fantasy. They might be able to make this more appealing by saying they don't want you to waste any time interviewing them for a low-paying position. While it sounds nice, it is not something that you need to be concerned about. The only thing you're getting in exchange is a less aggressive negotiation stance. If they ask for this information, you can reply with the following answer:

"I don't want to share that, I want focus on the value and ensuring it is a match. OR "I'm looking for a job that's a good fit for my skillsets and interests. I want the match to be good and I will focus on what I have to offer.

Keep it simple and to-the-point. Don't be afraid to do the right thing in everything that you do. You can make or break this answer by being confident and firm. It's open and honest, and it will likely bring an end to the discussion of money. It's not financially feasible to give up power at this point. This will happen after you have established rapport with the interviewers.

In these scenarios, it is possible that the interviewer doesn't respond immediately. This is a scenario that you will likely encounter throughout the whole process. If you don't want to hear it, silence can be very hard to handle. It is human nature to want more details and to respond. This is very harmful, especially when you run the risk of losing what you've said. You may feel the need give in and apologize. These are all bad things for your cause. These circumstances can make you look less confident. This is an area you should not show weakness before negotiations begin. This is where it's crucial to believe what you are stating. If you believe in your message and speak honestly and fairly, you can let your words stand. They'll move on very quickly, or push on, but the onus will be on them.

Let's pretend they do. They need to know the amount you want or are currently earning. This is an odd route they took. It goes against most social norms. It's unlikely but possible that this might be an issue. They could have many reasons to do so. There is no point in trying to list them all. The end result is the same regardless of what is holding you back. However, we will not give up.

Let's start with the scenario that they ask about your pay. No matter what question they ask, you should provide your total compensation as an amount in dollars. Don't simply give your salary. They might be tempted to make you pay less if they offer many benefits. Your salary should include bonuses, the value of any benefits, and any other incentives. This may include the cost of a company phone or car payment. This will provide you with a solid base from which to negotiate. This will allow you to be open and honest.

The second scenario is one that we'll be discussing. This can be done in several different ways. They are all very easy to accomplish. First, find out what the salary range for that position is. You can also ask them to describe the compensation that they believe is fair for the position. This will help you get them back on the right track. They may even give you an honest answer. This is an incredibly valuable service. It would be very difficult for them if they completely evade this question. You might be able, if you get an idea of their goal or range, to adjust your response.

When you are giving your number, however, it is best to have a range. When in doubt you will want to go high. It is possible to even go higher if you are given an indication that they are considering a higher number. It is important to prove that you can justify the amount. This can be achieved by citing relevant experience and skills. You must match these two with the desired attributes of a candidate.

This should be enough to get you through the majority the interview process. Still, you need to be successful in the interview. However, this will allow you to relax a bit more about the negotiation aspects of the interview. Keep in mind that you want them to believe in you. The more you can get to know them, the better. You should not delay talking about money. But, it cannot be delayed forever.

Chapter 13: Types Of Negotiation In Corporate

Negotiation involves the exchange of information between two or more people to reach an agreement that is mutually beneficial. Negotiation refers to the process of weighing all aspects of a situation and reaching an agreement that benefits everyone. Individuals put forth every effort in negotiations to reach an understanding that is mutually beneficial to all. It's also known as "bartering" in simpler terms.

Corporates can use a variety to increase productivity and improve employee relations.

Let's take an in-depth look at the different types negotiation:

Daily Negotiation: We negotiate at work with our superiors, or with our coworkers in order to make sure that everything runs smoothly. These are known by the "day-today negotiations".

Employee-supervisor-negotiation: A workplace; an employee must negotiate with their superiors to ensure that they are assigned responsibilities aligned with their interests and specialization. Accept any situation that makes you feel uncomfortable. Talk to your boss. Let's assume your boss asked you to prepare an organization's branding report and marketing strategies report. Accept the assignment only if requested by your boss. If your boss directs you to, negotiate with him. To avoid conflicts and misunderstandings in the future, it is better if you negotiate right away. To avoid any future conflict, an individual should negotiate his or her salary with the prospective employer before accepting any offer. Work will never be fun if it isn't what you want. Accepting work offers just because you need them is not a wise decision. It is best to negotiate carefully before joining any organization.

Negotiation among colleagues. This is vital for reducing the possibility of conflict or disagreements. One team member shouldn't feel overloaded while the others relax. You should have a good relationship with your coworkers, and only accept the responsibilities you are capable of. The entire burden of reaching targets should not rest on one person. It should be distributed equally among all. It is important to communicate with your team members and accept new responsibilities. If you'd like to take a day off, let a team member cover your work. You can also help your colleague during a leave of absence.

Negotiation enhances the team's output as well as the organization's overall productivity. By achieving what people expect, misunderstandings, and conflicts are reduced significantly, making the office a more pleasant environment.

Commercial negotiations: In most cases, commercial negotiations take place in the form contracts. Two people sit at the same table and discuss their issues. They then agree on acceptable terms. These situations should be a clear sign of agreement. Both parties sign a contract agreeing to follow its terms.

Cherry represented the administration department of a well-respected organization. He was charged with procuring bulk laptops through a vendor to the office's employees. Cherry asked for a quote from his vendor. Cherry discovered that the vendor's quoted price was far beyond the company budget. Cherry met up with the vendor to negotiate the price. Both parties came to an agreement over a price they could both accept. Cherry and her vendor signed a contract setting out the payment terms and payment methods, delivery date and warranty information. Most commercial negotiations involve an outside party. It is therefore necessary to create a contract to protect the interests of all parties.

Legal Negotiation. This is where an individual and the law negotiate. The individual must follow all regulations and rules established by the legal systems. The legal system does not disregard the individual's rights and interests.

Negotiations are essential in the workplace. They ensure that everyone feels included and satisfied. This also reduces conflict between coworkers.

Negotiation: Role of personality

An authoritative personality with good communication skills is essential for effective negotiation. Charming personalities are essential for effective negotiations.

Let's see how our personal traits influence negotiation effectiveness.

When negotiating, it is important for individuals to be authentic.

Don't deceive people or pretend you are someone you aren't. If you aren't satisfied with the transaction, don't pretend to. It is better if you express your concern right away than to wait. It is better to keep your mind at ease and relax, so that everything falls into place.

It is vital to be sincere as opposed to being serious.

Sincerity in negotiation is essential. Effective negotiation requires sincerity. Nothing should be taken for granted. Make sure you prepare well for the negotiation for a business sale and that you research all details of the transaction beforehand. The plan of the negotiation must be clearly understood by you. All necessary documents are essential for negotiations. Don't travel just for the sake.

Honesty is the best policy. Honesty during negotiations is vital. Never alter one's salary to gain a promotion at another company. You should not tell lies just for the sake of making money. Fear of being apprehended will always be present. It would reflect on your face. Don't be afraid; you will most likely receive what is due to you.

It is not a good idea to go to the shopkeeper if the laptop will be more expensive than you expect. He is not a foolish businessman. Be aware that he is also very attentive to the prices set by his fellow shopkeepers. It is better to ask the shopkeeper for discounts or extra accessories than to lower the price.

When negotiating, it is important to be well dressed. An unattractive person will find it hard to convince another person if they dress badly.

You must remember that the first impression will be your lasting impression.

How will you feel when you interact with a shopkeeper dressed casually, half asleep, or not at all? You won't bother to pay attention to him.

Jack wore a tee shirt and jeans to a business conference. Jack wore a t-shirt and jeans to a business meeting. The other side assumed Jack was not interested in the transaction and declined to participate in negotiations. Smart dressing does mean not dressing extravagantly. It is about dressing appropriately for what you are doing. Formal wear is preferred for business meetings. Don't forget about polishing your shoes to give it a polished look. People notice what your shoes look like.

Be patient: It has been shown that impatient people are poor negotiators. Do not think that asking for a $4 price on an item will make the shopkeeper agree immediately and then give it to them. You must convince him. This requires patience. You are not allowed to lose control and yell at the man.

Be flexible and encourage compromise. While it's acceptable to prioritise your personal interests, one should not be selfish. If you are the first person to accept something, it will not affect your significance or make you feel less important. However, it will help you to look up to the other person and gain everything you desire.

Effective negotiation is possible only if one has faith in the other side. Many people are helpful and kind, even though they may not be evil. One should never assume that another person intends harm. The second person is only there for business purposes; he's not your enemy. Instead of just getting to the point, make sure you start the conversation with a smile. If he wears a nice shirt, it is a good idea to compliment him. Consider him a friend. Never be arrogant. He represents his company like you. Place an online order for coffee and snacks. It will help to break down the ice and strengthen the bonds between the two of you. You should not be too casual, friendly, or informal.

You should maintain a professional attitude: After the transaction is closed, both parties should sign the contract in their presence. The minutes of the meeting should be distributed to all parties in order for clarity. Make sure you pay the shopkeeper after you have finished shopping. Rely also on nonverbal communication.

Effective negotiation requires you to be more attentive to your opponent. He may have an interesting idea that you can also benefit from. Do not assume the opposing party is ignorant. He too has been well prepared. Never underestimate the opponent. You should not disregard the shopkeeper when you shop. Instead, listen to his advice and then make a decision about what to buy.

Try to be diplomatic and tactful. There is a significant difference between these two. Intelligent people must know when to talk and when to stop speaking. Analyze what is happening and react accordingly. Your boss may ask you to say something, but it is not a reason to speak up. React appropriately and use your brain. If you think your statements will be considered foolish in a certain situation, it is best to stay silent.

Chapter 14: Setting The Agenda

Negotiators can't be effective unless they have a common understanding of the content and purpose of negotiations, as well as why it is being held. Although it may seem obvious to many, misinterpretations about the contents or purpose of negotiations are a common source of difficulty.

The local trade union branch approached an insurance company's personnel manager to request a meeting to 'examine the unsatisfactory condition in the computer area.'

Because of past complaints about ventilation, it was assumed that the request also refers to environmental problems. As such, he organized for the building engineers to do a series if temperature and humidity checks.

humidity. He began the meeting by acknowledging that there have been past problems but that recent checks had confirmed that the current environment is stable. It was.

It was discovered that the trade association wanted to talk about the layouts of desks/VDUs. This was in addition to their concerns about possible reorganization, which had been made worse by seeing an engineer in the area. The trade union side became suspicious of the intentions of the management and the personnel manager caused a negative impact on the discussion.

It would have been a smart move for the personnel manger to have clarified what the topic was before the meeting. It would have been even better if he had invited the trade union first to speak when the meeting started.

Agenda-setting can be broken down into two distinct aspects:

* Formally defining what the discussion is and agreeing with each other.

* Informally influencing content and character.

The formal agenda

Even though negotiation can be informal, like when two managers meet to talk about a matter of mutual concern, the effective manager decides what the subject should be.

It is all in advance.

Ed, an experienced and wily personnel manager (see the previous chapter), was well aware of these facts and would often try get an edge by initiating meetings without explaining his true reasons. One example: When he wanted to secure the financial director's approval to a budgetary modification, he called the director and said, "May I drop in on your this afternoon?" I have a question and need your guidance.

The finance director had previously agreed to the scheme until he noticed the ploy. However, he was then confronted by an exceptionally well-prepared case and presented case for more than minor concessions.

To such a request, the director would say: "What's it about?" I'm very busy today, so it would be helpful if you could take a few moments to call me now and let me know what's going on.

At the formal level, the topic matter of negotiations can often be so important that it may even be the subject for negotiation.

Sometimes media commentators make derogatory remarks about the time involved in national trade unionism disputes or in international diplomacy via 'talks around talks'. It may seem like a time-wasting activity but it can be crucial to the outcome of the final negotiation. An example of a subsidiary issue in an industrial relation dispute is the firing of unofficial striking members. Both sides may desire to progress in the wage talks. However, the trade union is keen to talk about the reinstatement the dismissed employees as precondition. Employers insist that these dismissals will not be reversed.

There is only one way to end the deadlock: have discussions about what needs to be discussed. And maybe, involve a third person to help these discussions.

In commercial negotiations or collective bargaining at company levels, a simple exchange is all that's required. A meeting will be scheduled and the initiator will write to the other with the following: "This letter confirms our arrangement to meet (date/time, place) to discuss subject (with a view towards reaching agreement about [objective]". Any possible misunderstandings regarding the nature of the meeting will be addressed by telephone or in writing. The purpose of all negotiations is to reach a mutual understanding of the goals.

Influencing Agenda

The ability to directly influence the tone of a meeting and the order in which the various aspects are discussed has an advantage for the main speaker of a negotiation session. This advantage is usually seized upon by the party initiating a claim or request. In other words, it is logical that they open the proceedings with a statement of their case. It does not mean they should be allowed introduce other issues than the ones already discussed, but it does allow them to have a significant influence on how the conversation will progress - the informal schedule.

If one is looking to establish the scene, rather then just responding, it is a good idea to claim this opening role. The other party must also be granted the right to open formal negotiations. There are ways to avoid the role of being reactive.

Ed's usual method of starting a negotiating meeting with his trade union officers is an example of this:

Ed had agreed to meet with the union after they had filed a claim for an increased overtime premium. A meeting like this would be opened by management by turning to the leader of the trade union and saying: 'We're meeting to look at your claim for higher overtime pay. Could you please explain your claim?'

This was not Ed's preferred way. He preferred to be first. So, his opening statement was "We are meeting today to discuss your overtime claim. Therefore, we will ask you to bat in the first. To make it easier for everyone to see, I'd suggest that you draw the background before we begin. He briefly spoke to the union about the past overtime arrangements as well as current overtime costs. He suggested that a combined study of unit costs might prove useful in preparing for any change. The phrase "before they start" did not prevent management from making an immediate objection.

It is possible to use a similar strategy in managerial discussions. If the finance director is confronted by Ed who has a well-prepared budget proposal, Ed can stop Ed from dictating how the meeting proceeds.

Despite initial efforts at influencing the agenda, negotiations can often become mired in a confusing discussion, which leads to arguments becoming repetitive, or losing sight of what each party is trying to achieve. This is often the case when one party has strong feelings about the topic at hand and becomes more concerned to express these feelings than it is with working towards a solution.

Three questions are helpful in these circumstances to bring the negotiations under control:

* "We fully understand your views about this issue, but we are not asking you to do anything."

* 'Are our right to think that x is the main point we should be considering?

* "Is it clear that our main point is y?"

Points of interest

* To make negotiations effective, all parties need to have a common understanding on what is to discussed and why.

* Agreements must be made on the subject and scope of the negotiations before they begin.

* This should be done in writing to define the agenda for formal negotiations.

* The first speaker is an important influence on the outcome of a negotiation.

* A brief rehearsal of the background is an effective way to get this opening job before fully negotiating.

* Confused negotiation need to be re-focused by a restatement (of each party's key points).

Chapter 15: Daily Exercise Benefits

Regular exercise can be good for your health and help you maintain a healthy weight. However, regular exercise can also have many other benefits for busy professionals. Regular exercise is known to release hormones that can improve your mood, reduce stress, increase sleep quality and, if done in the mornings, help you jump-start your work day. Exercising can improve productivity at work and, ultimately, your business' success. Here are some examples to show how regular exercise can be beneficial for your health and professional career.

Improve Your Network

Aside from networking functions and meeting new people through sports, going to the gym can also be a way to make connections. Golf is one way that many people use to grow their network. However, other sports can offer similar opportunities. The same thing can be said for the gym, as you will find others with similar interests and backgrounds to you. Exercise with others is a great way to share your personality and communicate in an entirely different manner than if it were done in a boardroom.

Goal setting and determination

If you're starting to exercise, or taking up a sport, set goals. You can encourage business professionals to use the same determination and drive you used to train for your marathon.

Increase your confidence

You will feel more confident when you work out and you achieve your workout goals. The satisfaction of completing a great workout can help improve your confidence in all areas of your day. You will feel great about the things you do.

Increase creativity and thinking skills

Exercise benefits more than your physical body. Studies have shown this to be true for your mental as well. Cardio exercise is not only beneficial for improving aerobic fitness, but it also helps improve cognitive function. This has been proven to be due to an increased blood flow to your brain.

Reduces Stress

When we're stressed we find it difficult to think clearly and act accordingly. We end up making many poor decisions at workplace. Through exercise, we can release endorphins which help to reduce stress. These endorphins give us a natural rush and make it easier to manage our day.

Energy level increases

For many people, working all day can cause fatigue. If you don't take action to combat fatigue, you can end up with low energy levels at work that can inhibit your performance. An experiment on the effect exercise has on one's energy levels showed that people who exercise daily saw a 20 percent increase in their energy levels. It also reduced their fatigue levels by 66%.

Regular exercise helps you not only stay awake through the day but it also improves your sleep quality at night. Here's a list of key reasons exercising is vital for busy professionals. If you are struggling to exercise, or if your routine is not set up properly, it can be daunting to reap the health benefits we have mentioned. A plan is the best way to get into a routine with exercise.

Here are some steps that you can take.

Goal Setting

Set your individual goals. It could be anything you want, such as losing weight or learning a new hobby. Whatever the reason, you need to make a list and then focus.

You can choose your workout times

Find a time that is convenient for you to work out and choose the best time to do it. Many people like to exercise first thing in the day, while others prefer evening work outs. If you work in an office that has a gym or a pool, you might be able to squeeze in some exercise during lunch. Your schedule and preferences will determine what you prefer. Listening and observing your body is an important habit to form. If you feel tired, sore, or if your body is still recovering from an exercise, you should stop the workout that day. You can always start over when you feel better.

Choose an Exercise

After setting your goals and deciding on a workout time, it's now time to choose the right workout. It could be as simple a jog, or walking. Swimming is another popular, easy-to-do exercise. Working professionals often choose to sign up at the local gym for yoga or aerobic classes. Are you ready to lift those weights? Do you not know where to start? You can get a personal coach to guide you through the basic movements. It is crucial to pick an activity that you enjoy and can keep going with.

Learn how to have fun

Once you have gone over all the details, the most important thing is to have a lot of fun doing the exercise. Make sure you're not bored by the activity you choose. Exercise should be fun. If you are energized and keep going, it will make you less likely to give in. Consider joining a class to get motivated and to keep you engaged.

Chapter 16: How To Avoid Screwing Up A Negotiation

You can learn guaranteed negotiation strategies to get what your heart desires. Many people fail to learn these techniques and make it a losing battle.

Do not waste your efforts trying to obtain a deal and end up spending a lot of time and money. Learn how to avoid common pitfalls in negotiations and you'll soon be a pro in this area.

1. Do not enter into a negotiation until you know what you want

If you don't know your needs, there is no point in trying to negotiate. Negotiation begins when both of the parties want to reach an arrangement. Your goal is to purchase a boutique and the saleslady's aim to sell it. If both goals are combined, they can become an agreement on making a sale. Before you go into the boutique, you already know your needs.

The other party cannot negotiate a nonexistent goal if they don't know what the store has or what it sells. If there is no product for sale, you can't haggle.

2. Do not give a range

If you are negotiating a sale, do not give a range of prices, dates, figures, or capacities. When you negotiate with a customer for your product you don't say "I will offer this to you for $5000-1,000" or "We are offering this for $5000-1,000." If the price is lower, no one will ever buy it. Don't let the deal breaker get out of hand.

3. Be confident in your offer and don't show indecisiveness.

Indecisiveness, uncertainty and indecisiveness are signs that you are still able to make a deal. This will give the impression that you are losing your mind and that the negotiation has reached an impasse.

Such words as "I'll be thinking about it" and "We'll look into what I can" can translate to "I still can do something to satisfy your conditions."

4. Do not give the customer the first price

One school of thought believes that the seller should let customers set the prices to win the pricing war. But, a Northwestern Kellogg School of Management systematic consumer study revealed that the opposite is much more likely to happen. The truth is that bidding goes on faster when someone throws a price.

When the seller makes the first move, the final sale price tends not to be as high as when the customer specifies the price.

5. You should not make the impression that you have the final say

It does not matter if your role is that of the decision maker. If you tell the opposite party that you are the final point in the negotiation process, they will do everything possible to make you feel uncomfortable. You will be in a dead end if you declare that you make the final decisions.

Be open if you are the negotiator. If you are truly the boss, be honest and say you still have partners or investors to consult.

6. Don't forget patience when you negotiate

Opposing negotiators can verbally intimidate negotiators - that is, you - especially if they know that they are the potential revenue, the money, and sales. There are also many insensitive people around that you might be able to have a conversation with. If you refuse to take in every offensive word spoken on your face you won't reach an agreement.

Take the destination in mind when you negotiate. It is possible for the journey to go wrong, but as long a you can make a deal, it will be a good thing.

Chapter 17: Probing The Other Side's Case

There are three important things to remember once negotiations are in progress:

* That the ultimate goal of any negotiation or resolution is to reach an agreed-upon outcome.

*... before making concessions should be thoroughly probed or tested by the other party (and possibly weakened)

*...every reasonable opportunity should not be missed to enhance one's own position.

Every chapter of this book has the first point. This chapter addresses the second of these points: the need to validate the position of the other side. The next chapter is about strengthening your case.

Exposing flaws

It is rare for any one party in negotiations to have a case that is unanswerable. However, negotiators are more likely to believe this and it is more common to present arguments worthy of immediate acceptance. Flaws can be caused by intentional distortions, poor preparation, or an unintentional assumption of right. Negotiators are often too convinced by their own arguments. This is why it is so important that both parties thoroughly examine the arguments.

The following are key points to remember:

Factual errors

You should not allow statements like "10% of deliveries have arrived two days late" and "increases on clerical salaries have fallen behind RPI rise" to be ignored. These statements can be important in negotiations. The party making them should be asked to provide hard evidence to support them.

Omissions

It is normal for negotiators not to have complete but accurate data when building a case. So while 10% of deliveries may have been late or not at all, the analysis period also included the unmentioned railroad strike that distorted the statistics. Negotiators need to be honest with themselves and the other side. What other facts are possible to be relevant?

In a national negotiation concerning fire service salaries, figures were given about the number long-serving firefighters who had resigned from the service in the preceding six months. This was used to support the claim that men are leaving the service because they don't get enough pay. However, figures for the equivalent resignations rates over the last five years were not provided. These numbers were available and it was obvious that there had never been a significant, recent increase in the resignation rate.

Incorrect use of statistics

Most statistics are misused in two ways. One, they can be used to give averages of very few cases. Two, averages can be used to conceal very large variations of actual data. "The average time taken to complete a special production was 28 hours. This was against your contractual commitment of 20 hours. But how many special-production runs were there in total? Some production runs were not enough to ensure that the average was reliable.

Another possibility is that the average was grossly distorted due to a single 90-hour case. It is important to question averages (or arithmetic medians) often by asking details about the number, range and mode positions.

In a commercial agreement about office rental, one party claimed that the rents on equivalent premises in their area had risen to PS32/sq feet. The other party proved that while this figure was mathematically accurate, it was not inclusive of a range of PS20 - PS70. In addition, the median figure was only PS27. It was affected by two exceptionally high rentals, which were found on 28 of the premises.

Failure of logic

Many firms draw firm conclusions from weak base. "Salaries are too low due to staff leaving for higher-paying jobs elsewhere" - this is normal. Also, unless the company in which one works is the highest paying, there will always have other companies that pay more. Any major conclusion that the other party draws must be checked against the foundation on which it was drawn.

Appeal to emotion

Negotiators are more likely to resort emotionally when there is a weak case. "OK, so the company lacks cash and is facing fierce competition overseas. However, it is not unfair that our members should get paid below the industrial median." "Wouldn't your business benefit from being seen to show generosity, even though our client does not have legal rights?" It is possible to have strong influences such as reputation and fairness. This can help justify cases which are otherwise weak. It does not mean you have to accept all such appeals. It is important to first recognize the argument and then analyze them rationally and critically before making concessions.

If you want to find flaws in the argument of the other side, it is better to ask questions rather than respond with counter-statements. Questions are less intimidating, but they can be more open and transparent. It is easier to ask questions, even if the answers are known, than to say: 'On what cases is your average number? To answer the question "On how many instances is your average figure based?" it's more effective than to simply state that "Your average figure doesn't mean anything." The direct questioning of facts (how much?) is not enough. how much? when? You can also ask these general but very useful probing questions:

* Could that be explained more fully?

* We don't agree with your logic. Could you suggest a different approach?

* Is this not what you really mean? If it is, how can you justify?

* Could your explanation of the connection between x/y be given?

Validating credibility

It would be wrong if you suggested that in all negotiations, it should be attempted to undermine authority from the leader of the other party. His or her standing among the team's members might be quite high. Any attempt at demeaning them would be counter-productive. The team will rally for their leader.

However, there may be occasions when a vocal, probably aggressive team leader doesn't have the unquestioned support from his or her colleagues. It's worthwhile to put any faults in the team leader's case directly on the leader. The team's confidence and trust in their leader can be undermined, and they will have a harder time achieving their original negotiating goals. This is evident in an industrial relationship example.

A trade union group met with management in order to file a claim for reinstatement of an employee who had been dismissed because of a disciplinary offence. The trade team was made up of a strongly opinionated district official and five less assertive shop-stewards. The district official was the only one talking. He adopted a uncompromising stance that was supported, he claimed, in part by case law arising as a result of a recent Employment Appeals Tribunal ruling. His team clearly appreciated his knowledge of the law. Management allowed the argument for reinstatement, based on the legal position, to be made, even though the issue was influenced almost exclusively by local considerations.

The personnel manger then decided it was the right moment to tell George, "You would be wrong in your argument." George, the only problem is that your case law is outdated. Did you know that they overturned their Employment Appeals Tribunal ruling last week? I have the report here for you if you would like to view it. This was a serious blow to the confidence of shop stewards in their district officials' competence.

The innocent question: 'Are we sure about that? This powerful method can be used to cast doubts on the credibility of opposing negotiators. This can be helpful if they can provide evidence to back up their claims, but it can cause damage to their confidence and credibility in the eyes of their colleagues if their arguments are flawed.

Points of interest

* The case of the opposite side should be examined:

Factual errors and omissions

Statistical misuse

Failure of logic

They have an emotional appeal.

* Sometimes, the leader of one side's side might need to be undermined. However, this should not cause a defensive reaction.

Chapter 18: Negotiation Strategies

The term "strategy", which originated in ancient Greece, was translated as "the arts of a commander". Even though the meaning of strategy is broader today, it can be summarized as follows: Strategy is the main model for action.

When we talk about a strategy, we mean the actions we will undertake to achieve our desired outcome. Your success or failure to reach your goal will directly affect the strategy you choose. It's interesting to note that, in certain situations, the negotiation strategy may be aimed directly at achieving the desired goal at any cost. In others, it might be at maintaining relations among opponents. In third, it might be at adapting and overcoming the circumstances of a stronger adversary.

The most popular and well-known classification of negotiation strategies is WIN-WIN. It was developed by Harvard negotiators

— William Urey (Bruce Patton), Roger Fisher (Roger Fisher) and later presented as Negotiating Without Failure: The Way to Consent. By the way, WIN-WIN strategy looks very similar with the Thomas Kilman grid. This is a classification that distinguishes five styles in conflict behavior: Compromise and Adaptation, Rivalry as well as Compromise, Compromise and Compromise.

These are the four main negotiation strategies that can be used to distinguish this classification based on its main premises:

* WIN-WIN Strategy (COOPERATION)

* WIN-LOSE Strategy (COMPETITION)

* Strategy "LOSE-WIN" (ADAPTATION)

* LOSE-LOSE Strategy (DODGE)

This or that strategy must be determined using two parameters: the values of the relations and of the result

Let's look in greater detail at each strategy.

WIN-WIN Strategy (COOPERATION)

The WIN/WIN strategy is based upon cooperation. It is designed for all negotiators to win. The basic idea behind this strategy is to ensure that the opposing parties understand, respect, take into account and share each other's interests. It is worth noting, that this strategy is considered to be the most successful in any negotiation. This is why it is essential to try and find common ground.

EXAMPLE. Sam was in the same company as John. Both of them strived to achieve career growth and were competitive with each other. John, much like Sam, was determined to stand out, distinguish himself, and to gain a higher position in the company. Opponents came up a number of promising projects, and they were successful in realizing them. The company's position was improving and the head was pleased with this. One day, however, a new leader came into the company. The new leader didn't know that

John and Sam had planned a "race". They were assigned the task of working together on a common project. The business, as you might expect, was successful. The project was not able to move forward due to the fact that each opponent wanted to prove they were better than each other. The newly appointed leader saw a drop in the ratings of colleagues, and he suggested to them that they may soon be fired. John and Sam were forced together to finish the task. Colleagues began looking for ways to work together and not "jumping up" to each other. They found it quite comfortable to work together to pool their talents and knowledge. John and Sam got the desired result and were eventually promoted to leadership positions.

WIN-LOSE Strategy (COMPETITION)

The WIN/LOSE strategy, also known as VICTORY-DEFEAT, uses competition to its foundation. It is about winning by the opponent, who makes the best effort to do so. The second opponent will be regarded as the enemy and even the enemy. This strategy is usually used in situations when the result is more important than the relationship. Participants who follow such strategies are able to use every method possible to achieve their goals. If you don't reach such extremes then the strategy will be very effective in the sales field, where the seller is trying to increase his profit margins by selling more or less expensive goods. A rivalry strategy is usually only useful for short-term purposes.

EXAMPLE. The sales manager of an electronics retail store is given the task of fulfilling a plan for one month. However, at the end of the month, the seller realizes that he is far from fulfilling the plan. This means that his work could be in danger. The seller takes the decision to go ahead and fulfill the plan. Because the seller's future relationships with customers are not too worrying, he can start to offer customers the most pricey products or a lot of related products. If the seller shows kindness and communicates well with customers so that they can't refuse, it will be possible to fulfill the plan. But the likelihood of these buyers returning to the seller in future is low.

LOSE-WIN Strategy (ADAPTATION)

The "LOSE" strategy ("DEFEAT–VICTORY") uses the device to its foundation. In negotiation, the opportunistic strategies leads to the conscious loss of the participant who chose it as well as the victory of his adversary. This strategy is most useful in situations in which the relationships between opponents are very important.

EXAMPLE. The manager of small company wants to sign with a big company a contract so that his company is its partner. In the beginning, he relies upon certain conditions, creates a contract and hopes to get a certain outcome. During negotiations, however, a representative representing a large firm says that a deal can be signed, but only if the terms of his business are better than those the manager for a small company. Even though the conditions in the manager's contract were not satisfactory, he still signed it. This is because his company has good prospects even with these negative conditions.

LOSE-LOSE Strategy (DODGE)

The "LOSELOSE" strategy ("DEFEATDEFEAT") is based on evasion. The strategy is most commonly used in negotiations by parties in weak positions. There are some situations when one or both of the parties deliberately causes mutual loss. Another option is to use the evasion technique when the rivals don't want to agree to each another, regardless of how the negotiations end.

EXAMPLE. A person who is not well-versed in Internet technology visits a resource for web design. He intends to order a website for his online store. The developers listen to customer requirements, determine the best option for him, and give the price. The customer is happy, the transaction has been completed, and prepayment has been sent. The customer begins to wander the Internet and discovers that an easy way to create a website for a store online is possible in just a few minutes and absolutely free. The customer becomes panicky, believing that he had been tricked and that all is not well. The customer who had paid the prepayment made to the developers agrees to reimburse them. He calls to request a website from the company. The developers fail to meet the demands of the customer and return the money. Furthermore, the customer, having "saved", money can be used to hire a friend (or even to "make a website") or to go to a developer who is more affordable. This means that the customer will now be able to learn all about creating sites over a long period of time. Or, he or she will receive help from a skilled specialist. The customer is now the second loser. While the customer will in the end come to his own conclusions and realize why the studio is making money, it won't be too late.

So now we have looked at the key negotiation strategies. The particular situation and its context will determine the type of strategy that you should use. You need to be aware of the information you will receive during the preparation stage for negotiations as well as the significance of the relationship and outcome. If you want to achieve your goal first, you can choose a Rivalry plan. However, if he is already well prepared for negotiations and seeing you compete with him, he may decide to follow the Evasion or Adaptation strategy. This could adversely impact your standing as a negotiator.

If maintaining a healthy relationship is important to you and you are open to giving up your goals, the Adaptation strategy could be the right choice. It is not easy because your opponent may begin to actively pressure, noticing that you are "giving up" and not attaching much importance to your relationship with them. As a result, you could find yourself in a far worse position than you first thought.

There may be many possible outcomes to events. Therefore, it is crucial that you plan and prepare for all negotiations. It will be useful to remember the flexibility, feedback and planning we spoke of earlier. You can always find out what the opponent's negotiation strategy is. Flexible behavior in emergency situations will let you modify individual elements and make changes to your strategy.

Last, but not least, I think the Cooperation Strategy is the best strategy. Because it allows both the negotiating parties and their respective goals to be achieved without significant losses (or sometimes without them), and also helps them maintain and strengthen relationships that can lead to future effective cooperation.

Strategies are crucial, and they can help us learn how to negotiate, even though they have a very high importance. This is exactly the topic we'll be covering in the next lesson.

Chapter 19: Negotiating With Your Boss

Negotiating with your boss is the hardest part of any negotiation. Your boss may be in a different position than you, but he is the one who will put food on your table. This can make it difficult for you and make you afraid. Even worse, if he gets on the wrong side of you, he could fire you. Your boss will appreciate your professionalism and tactfulness when negotiating. To be successful, you must do it correctly. These steps are helpful.

Step 1 – Be certain about the outcome you desire to negotiate

Before you agree to negotiate, ensure that you have a legitimate reason. You must be clear about your goals and prepare for negotiations. What will your boss gain from your offer Remember that your boss must get something from it. While preparing your arguments, it is important to think about the personality of your boss.

Let's imagine you want a raise.

Common minimum wage applicable to personnel within your industry.

Benefits received by other people in the same rank you are

Minimum wage as required by law in the area you live in

Hours of duty

Your boss may offer you benefits

Your job specifications

Job descriptions of workers who hold the same position in different companies

How your boss, and the company, can benefit from you offer

Justification for your request for a raise

Make sure you have the following facts in mind when preparing your talk points. Prioritize which statement should be the first. It may be a good idea to take a summary of all your arguments with you during negotiation. It is important to memorize your opening statements. This will help to calm your nerves and increase self-confidence.

Step 2: Select the timing

Although you are well-prepared, it is difficult to manage your time. A raise is impossible to request at the end if everyone is too busy writing reports or evaluating the events of the previous year. You should ask for a raise after the personnel evaluations are complete, which usually occurs before the start of the next fiscal year.

You can focus on your performance if you've received a raise. Be sure to check with your boss that he is also happy and willing to listen. Consider whether your company can afford to increase you salary. Maybe the company is experiencing a financial crisis and cannot meet your demands. If this is the situation, you will have wait until a more favorable time.

It is preferable to tell your boss ahead of time about your plans, so he can adjust the schedule accordingly. Surprising meetings are not always appreciated, especially in busy workplaces.

Step #3: Present your case

Be sure to prepare your presentation so that your employer's goals align with yours. Do not allow emotions to dictate your presentation. Instead present the facts to back up your request. These facts need to be documented and noted. So that your boss has a second copy, prepare two copies.

PowerPoint slides are a great way to present your points/case. This will help you focus your points better. You can highlight what you want to stress.

Be confident and clear in your communication. Be polite and straightforward. To help ease your nervousness before the meeting, you may perform the breathing exercises in chapter 3, to relax.

Your ACOA, Alternative Course of Action (Course of Action) must always be ready in the event of rejection.

Any suggestions or questions you receive from your boss, listen carefully. Answer honestly, and then take the time to note any suggestions.

Step #4 - Find a compromise

If your initial proposal doesn't get accepted, negotiate with your boss for a compromise. Don't abandon your boss. Discuss with him the ACOA. Be prepared to modify your proposals and accept some of his suggestions. Remember that negotiation is an act of collaboration. Consider working with him to reach an acceptable agreement for both of you.

Step #5 -- Document the final agreement

You should document everything that happened during the negotiations. This can be signed jointly by you. This temporary proof will be used to confirm what you have agreed upon while the formal document in its final form is being prepared.

Step #6 -- Shake hands

After the negotiation, greet your boss and say hello. Your boss will see you as a positive person if you show good manners and good conduct after you have achieved what your boss wants.

A lot of preparation is required before you ask for a raise. Prepare yourself for this.

Conclusion

Most people have already known what you have just learned. You may have it hidden in your heart, waiting to be discovered. It is strange how we forget simple things we knew all along. It is easy to forget what is crucial in today's fast-paced and self-focused world. We want to go beyond being more persuasive. We strive to build the mysterious trait of character. You are likely to have an intuitive understanding of the majority of the contents of this book. Below I have condensed them so that you can quickly look at them. I consider them to be life tools and not a means of getting anything you want from anyone.

Making a first impression is vital. Don't be afraid to stand tall. Your first meeting will determine how you are perceived. The first impression that you leave will last the longest.

Make your body language more friendly: Smile. Make eye contact. These techniques make you more trustworthy and more self-confident. Fake it if needed

It is important to understand the arguments you are fighting: Pay attention. Assess not just what is being spoken but also the general mood amongst others. Encourage agreement with positive reinforcement, and remember to include people from the outside. Keep your cool when you disagree.

Your argument should be understood thoroughly. Also, you should be prepared to defend the weaknesses of your argument. Know the perspective of the opponent. The positive points in your situation should be highlighted. Always strive to improve your communication skills and use of language.

You must be prepared to lose some battles. Keep the bigger picture in mind, and don't be afraid to lose. Never compromise your credibility to get a point. Your most powerful weapon? Your credibility

Since you already know everything, you'll only need to review this chapter from time to time or before any important meetings. As with any skill, persuasion must be practiced frequently if it is to grow. However, since they are already part & parcel of your being, it won't take long before they become part of your daily life. You will quickly discover that the more you are seen as a powerful and influential person, the more you will be asked to do these tasks. As you become more calm and competent in persuading others, I believe that this will happen.

CPSIA information can be obtained
at www.ICGtesting.com
Printed in the USA
BVHW052246090223
658263BV00007B/226

9 781774 856383